BERLI

C000151587

WALT DISNEY WORLD and ORLANDO

- A ✓ in the text denotes a highly recommended sight
- A complete A–Z of practical information starts on p.115
- Extensive mapping throughout: on cover flaps and in text

Printed in Switzerland by Weber SA, Bienne.

1st edition (1995/1996)

Although we make every effort to ensure the accuracy of the information in this guide, changes do occur. If you have any new information, suggestions or corrections to contribute, please write to Berlitz Publishing at the above address.

Text:	Martin Gostelow
Editor:	Sarah Hudson
Photography:	Martin Gostelow, except p.33, 105 Jacques Bétant; pp.4, 6, 9, 61, 62 and 83 © Universal Studios Florida; p.7 © Busch Gardens, Tampa; p.10 © Orlando/Orange County Convention and Visitors Bureau Inc.; p.85 (inset) © Wet 'n' Wild
Layout:	Cristina Silva
Cartography:	Visual Image

Cover photographs: (front) Sea World – Martin Gostelow (© Berlitz)
(back) Universal Characters © Universal Studios Florida

CONTENTS

Orlando and the Theme Parks

Surely everyone has heard by now. Walt Disney World Resort, near Orlando in central Florida, is the biggest holiday attraction on earth.

Even if you aren't someone who likes to follow the crowd, don't let that put you off – there's plenty of room for everyone. After all, it's not a small world. The Disney property covers an area of 44sq miles (113sq km) or 28,000 acres (11,200ha), almost the size of San Francisco. Orlando isn't Walt Disney World, however, and Walt Disney World isn't Orlando. For one thing, the resort is situated some 25 miles (40km) south west of the city, and much nearer the once sleepy cattle town of Kissimmee. Mickey Mouse and his friends certainly triggered the boom, but lots of other attractions have clustered round as well, to benefit from the huge flow of visitors. The world's biggest supply of hotel beds, 120,000 at the last count, is ready and waiting to accommodate them.

Many visitors fly in directly to Orlando International Airport, whose traffic has multiplied by a factor of 20 in the years since the advent of Disney. Others arrive in Miami, 220 miles (353km) away to the south, with good roads and frequent flights to Orlando. In addition, huge numbers drive from all over North America – just check the licence plates of some of the cars in one of the parks and count the number of states represented. Train and bus services also link Orlando with the rest of Florida and with main US cities.

Walt Disney World opened its gates for the first time to the public on Friday, 1 October 1971, which was deliberately chosen as the quietest day in Florida's least busy month for tourism. Ready to learn from experience, the park's executives wished to avoid the traffic snarls and capacity crowds that had jammed California's Disneyland on its first day. **5**

*Y*our favourite cartoon characters come alive in the theme parks and even sign autographs.

slow progress: he meant that it would evolve and expand – and so it has proved. First there was the Magic Kingdom, a more ambitious version of Disneyland in California; then came the EPCOT Center, even bigger; and finally in 1989 the Disney-MGM Studios Theme Park added to the empire. All have grown since they opened, and there's talk of a fourth theme park by the end of the century. Initially there were three Disney hotels, now there are 12, offering anything up to 2,200 rooms each. Their designers are rewriting the book of resort architecture – they just don't know where to stop!

Walt Disney World is much more than an amusement park, or parks, and it's not just for children either. You might be surprised to learn that it's one of the most popular honeymoon destinations in the United States. In fact, the majority of its visitors are adults – for them Walt Disney World provides nightspots and bars in hotels as well as discos and clubs on Pleasure Island. With pools and sandy beaches (yes,

Even so, 10,000 visitors came. The day after Thanksgiving in late November the figure had risen to 60,000 and the park was full. Since then, Walt Disney World has grown in popularity each year.

Disney himself had prophesied that it would never be finished, but he wasn't predicting

6

this far from the sea), lakes and sailing, tennis courts, and more golf facilities than any Florida *golf* resort, you might stay within the Disney 'borders' for your whole trip. Only then you'll miss all the other attractions of the Orlando area.

Universal Studios Florida opened in 1990, but plans for studios here had been around for several years, ever since Orlando had gained its reputation as 'Hollywood East'. (Long enough in fact for Disney to get ahead and open Disney-MGM Studios first.) The idea of coming to central Florida was not simply to tap into the theme park market, but also to take advantage of the climate and to reduce labour and other costs. A 444-acre (178ha) site was selected

Park planners go to the ends of the earth for realism: 19th-century Africa comes to Busch Gardens.

north of International Drive, close to the key I-4 interstate highway. The open spaces offered the chance to build rides and attractions as well as the real production facilities on a huge scale. Sets were made as accessible to visitors as possible, so that they would become part of the show. Investment in Universal Studios by the joint owners, MCA and the Rank Organization, reached around $630 million, and when you see the size of the operation and some of the technology, you'll understand where all the money went.

Sea World began in Florida in 1973 as an up-to-date version of the marine parks which have been a Florida tradition ever since the 1920s. Now it has grown and developed into much more than leaping dolphins, clowning sealions and parading penguins. Busch Entertainment Corporation, part of the giant brewing empire Anheuser-Busch, bought Sea World in 1989, adding it to their already existing properties – Busch Gardens, Tampa, and Cypress Gardens, south of Orlando – and throwing down a challenge to Disney supremacy. They have multiplied the attractions and added to the

*H*aven't I seen you somewhere before? Lookalikes will turn up just about anywhere in the film studio theme parks.

variety, to make a visit to Sea World a logical part of any trip to Orlando.

After you've spent a few days in the theme parks, seen the impressively gaudy strip called International Drive, and driven up and down the I-4 and Highway 192 a few times, you may begin to wonder, but yes, Orlando *does* have a city centre, although millions who go straight from the airport to Walt Disney World or Kissimmee never see it. From the top of Disney's highest building, it's no more than a speck on the horizon. Even International Drive, halfway between, is about 9 miles (15km) from downtown Orlando.

Until the 1960s, this was an old-fashioned inland town in a flat landscape, dotted with lakes and swamps. True, it had several charming suburbs built by prosperous migrants who were retreating from northern winters, and it still has them, but all else has changed out of recognition. Firstly the space programme, based at nearby Cape Canaveral, attracted high technology industries to the region, then came the tourist boom, calling for huge numbers of people to work in the labour intensive service sector. They needed services too, and so began the chain reaction.

There's been a population explosion, and compared with

Old timers wouldn't know modern Orlando, standing where all was once swamp.

much of Florida, it's a younger crowd. Many big companies moved their headquarters here, and sports stars have made it their home, making Orlando the hub of central Florida, with mushrooming steel and glass towers and headlong development. Unsurprisingly, however, the above didn't lure many people away from the theme parks, so Orlando decided to inject some fun with an entertainment complex of its own, restoring several old buildings to create the food and entertainment complex of Church Street Station.

Excellent roads put all the attractions nearby within easy reach. In less than an hour's drive is the Atlantic Coast and Kennedy Space Center, with the Gulf Coast not much further away to the west. There's enough to occupy several holidays. What a dilemma! No wonder people keep returning.

The Walt Disney Story

Walter Elias Disney was born on 5 December 1901 in Chicago. His father was a building contractor of Anglo-Irish stock and Canadian birth.

When Walt was still a toddler, the whole family moved to a farm in Marcelina, Missouri. All the children, even the youngest, had to help on the farm, but Walt showed an interest in drawing from an early age and took his first art lessons in Kansas City when he was 14.

In 1919 he served as an ambulance driver with the US Army in France, too late for action in World War I. As surviving photographs show, he still drew during this period, though his talents were confined to caricatures on his ambulance and fake medals on his buddies' jackets.

He had seen the simple animated films of the time, and was sure he could do better. In Kansas City he teamed up with artist Ubbe 'Ub' Iwerks to make commercials and versions of Cinderella and Robin Hood. He formed a partnership with his older brother Roy to produce a series of shorts called *Alice in Cartoonland*, combining live action and animation (a formula Disney was to return to years later with *Mary Poppins*).

DISNEY GOES TO HOLLYWOOD

The *Alice* series enjoyed some success, but the costs broke the new studio. Disney picked himself up, packed his bags and moved to Los Angeles in 1923, determined to make animated films that were more than crude fillers. He wanted to create characters who had a life of their own and emotions that people could recognize. Iwerks joined him to look after the artwork and Roy Disney, who was already in California, ran the business side.

The pattern was soon set. Disney had the ideas and, as he explained, 'pollinated' the various departments, like a bee moving from flower to flower. By 1926 he had stopped drawing and he was sometimes embarrassed later when children assumed he had created his films singlehanded – and yet he couldn't do them a sketch of Pluto or Goofy. *Oswald the Lucky Rabbit* brought recognition, but Disney lost the rights to the character in a contractual dispute with a New York distributor. He learned his lesson: from then on he retained absolute control of his company's creations and defended them fiercely with copyrights and trademarks.

MICKEY MAKES HIS MARK

According to Disney, he was on a train back from New York when he came up with the idea of a new hero, a mouse to be called ... Mortimer! When he told his wife Lillian, she wisely suggested Mickey instead. Ub Iwerks drew him to Walt's satisfaction, with the famous circular ears, velvet trousers, big round-toed shoes and four-finger gloves.

It was 1927, and Mickey Mouse appeared in the silent film *Plane Crazy*, which came out at the same time as the first-ever talking picture *The Jazz Singer*. Sensing the way the wind was blowing, Disney quickly withdrew his film, and re-released it with a soundtrack. In 1928, Mickey starred in the first animated film with sound, *Steamboat Willie*. Walt himself was the provider of Mickey's falsetto voice (and continued in that role for many years). Minnie Mouse made her debut in the same film, when Mickey hauled her on board with a boathook.

FAME AND FORTUNE

Steamboat Willie and its stars were a huge success. In some countries the characters were given new names – in Italy Mickey was called Topolino – and it was no coincidence when the very same name was given to Fiat's popular car.

Disney's dream had come true. The sheer quality of the work, the attention to detail, the wit and talent of the artists and his own perfectionism had lifted animated films to new heights. He had the respect of film-makers who watched Disney productions for new ideas. The public loved them.

In 1934, Donald Duck's arrival brought a personality to counteract Mickey's essential **13** cheerfulness. The malicious, irascible bird in the silly sailor suit whose pride always led to a fall became an even bigger favourite than Mickey.

Disney was a pioneer in the use of colour, with *Flowers and Trees* in 1933, and some of the *Silly Symphony* series in the mid-30s. A taste of things to come, their stories were set in the kinds of fairy-tale landscape that sprang to life in the theme parks many years later.

SNOW WHITE

Now Walt Disney was ready to climb the ultimate mountain, even if the studio's accountants were alarmed at the cost. He was planning the first full-length animated feature film, *Snow White and the Seven Dwarfs*. It's hard now to imagine how daring a proposal this seemed – and was. To attain the quality he had in mind, very fine artwork was needed. In addition, an 83-minute film didn't use just ten times the drawings and painted 'cels' (see p.21) as an 8-minute film. Far *more* than that were needed to give the human characters the smooth movements of live actors. He hired 300 new artists (making 750) and the job still took over two years.

Finally, in late 1937, *Snow White and the Seven Dwarfs* was given a star-studded première in Hollywood, the first ever for an animated production. That first audience was enchanted and dissolved into laughter and tears as millions have done since. The film was a smash hit and won a special Academy award, a big Oscar for Snow White and seven little ones for the dwarfs. *Pinocchio* followed in 1940: an even more intricate achievement.

Also in 1940, Disney broke new ground again with *Fantasia*, setting beautiful, funny and bizarre scenes to the music of Bach, Beethoven, Tchaikovsky and Stravinsky. Mickey Mouse played *The Sorcerer's Apprentice*, whose delusions of omnipotence unleash forces beyond his control. It was almost a metaphor for the war that had begun in Europe and was about to enmesh the US. When it did, Disney Studios made training films, with GIs adopting the suitably aggressive Donald Duck in Commando uniform as a mascot.

BUILDING THE DREAM

After World War II, Disney made *Song of the South*, combining live action and animation. This was followed by a number of all-live films including *Treasure Island*, *Swiss Family Robinson*, and *20,000 Leagues Under the Sea*, which all generated ideas for the future theme parks. The animated feature films of the 1950s – *Cinderella*, *Alice in Wonderland*, *Peter Pan* and *Sleeping Beauty* – also served as inspiration for the theme parks.

Disney had always loved the idea of amusement parks, but by the time he came to visit them with his daughters, they had become tawdry and run-down. Worse still, they were unimaginative. Some operators were simply in it for a fast buck, others were downright dishonest, but since the 1930s Disney had thought of creating his own version.

By 1947, on doctors' orders, he was supposed to be relaxing a bit, but for Walt that just meant throwing himself into a new project, this time a model railway which got bigger and bigger, until he had no more room for it ... unless he built a theme park, of course; then he'd have all the space he needed. He presented the plan to his more cautious brother Roy, who wouldn't agree to invest more than $10,000 in the 'screwy idea'. As Walt Disney's story goes, he raised the capital himself, on his life insurance policy.

By 1952 he had set up a company, WED (his initials) and sketched out the plans. He acquired 160 acres (65ha) of land in Anaheim, on the southern edge of Los Angeles. Now he could not only build a railway, but a complete 'Disneyland', and people it with his characters. His designers created a huge stage set, on which visitors moved from scene to scene like stars of the show. It was more than a fairground, an adventure playground or an amusement park. There had never been anything like it.

It opened on 17 July 1955, an overwhelming success with over 4 million visitors in the first year, rising to 10 million a year as the fame spread. The number of attractions doubled and executives learned from experience how to handle such **15** unprecedented numbers. But Disney was not entirely happy. Fast-food and souvenir shops had spread to the borders of Disneyland, creaming off revenues he felt should belong to Walt Disney Productions.

A NEW WORLD IN FLORIDA

Disney was determined not to make the same mistake twice. When he began searching for a suitable theme park site in the eastern United States, one prerequisite was a great deal of space. The others were a year-round sunny climate and good travel connections that could expand to handle the traffic. The scouts found what he was looking for in central Florida, near the quiet market town of Orlando. Nominees started to buy land, eventually picking up 27,500 acres (11,000ha) by 1964 at the reasonable cost of $6 million, or about $2,200 per acre. If word had got out that Disney was behind it, prices would have rocketed. (When it did, they did, multiplying a hundredfold overnight).

Disney planned a park on the lines of Disneyland, except larger, but his dream went far beyond. He envisaged nothing less than a 'living, breathing city of the future', his 'Experimental Prototype Community of Tomorrow' – EPCOT. He outlined his plan in a film, but sadly, it was the last he was to make. In December 1966, he died quite suddenly, of complications following surgery for lung cancer.

Roy O Disney had not always seen eye-to-eye with his brother, but they had recently set aside their differences, and he became chairman of Walt Disney Productions. At his suggestion, the Florida project was given the name Walt Disney World – a generous tribute to his brother. ('Resort' was added to emphasize the range of activities.)

Preparation began in 1967 and construction followed in 1969. By October 1971, The Magic Kingdom was open and this time guests could stay in Disney hotels, swim, play golf and tennis, dine and be entertained without leaving Disney territory. When everyone from top executives to the newest cast member had to help park cars or cook hot-dogs, it began a tradition – cross-utilization, or 'X-U' in Disney parlance.

EPCOT took longer to realize. It was hard to reconcile a harmonious 'living community' with streams of visitors in their millions, but the Disney organization had gained a lot of experience at various World Fairs, and the EPCOT Center, opened in 1982, resembles a twin-centre World's Fair. Future World recalls the celebration of technology Disney had proposed, while World Showcase, comprising the pavilions of several nations, is quite different. But both are true to Walt's dictum: 'I would rather entertain and hope that people learn, than educate and hope they're entertained.'

Tokyo Disneyland followed in 1983 and was another hit. Soon the parks became more important than film-making. Believing that EPCOT's costs and the shortage of new film successes had weakened Walt Disney Productions, a takeover was planned. 1984 was a year of high drama. Perhaps it was just lucky that the 50th birthday of gutsy little Donald Duck coincided with the company's survival and a new era.

BACK ON TOP

As the dust settled, Michael Eisner became the chairman and chief executive and Frank Wells president. The Disney family connection continued when Roy E Disney, son of Roy O, became head of animation. The Disney organization was transformed with a string of film successes, new television series and fresh licensing contracts for Disney products. One of Eisner's first acts was to sign the agreement with the French which was to lead to the building of the Euro Disney Resort east of Paris: it opened in April 1992.

The attractions of Walt Disney World were increased with the 1989 openings of Typhoon Lagoon and Pleasure Island, and a *third* theme park celebrating the company's re-dedication to its roots, the movie business. Disney-MGM Studios has real film sets and TV studios where actual productions take shape and an animation department, which created long sequences for *Beauty and the Beast* and *Aladdin*, fulllength features in the tradition of Walt Disney's best. **17**

Where to Go

The Walt Disney World Resort

The Walt Disney World Resort contains *three* immense theme parks and several other major attractions which could almost rank as theme parks in their own right. Naturally, there's also plenty to do and see beyond Disney borders. Faced with so many possibilities, you will need a plan of action, especially if this is your first visit or your time is limited. How do you decide what to do, and the order in which to do it? We don't suggest a rigid schedule, but unless you allocate your time wisely, you'll find it difficult to take full advantage of all that's on offer.

Your first step is to abandon any idea of 'seeing everything'. With the help of this guide, choose which parks you want to visit and then the rides and attractions that most appeal to you. On pp.115-141 you will find general informa-tion on transport, first aid, lost property etc, but to begin with here are some hints on how to tackle Walt Disney World.

A FEW POINTERS

Peak times are Christmas and early January, the weeks before and at Easter, mid-June to late August, and long weekend holidays in the United States such as Thanksgiving in late November. Winter in central Florida is generally delightful, and it's hot and humid in the summer, but you can cool off in hotel pools and waterparks and enjoy spending more time outside in the evenings. There is really no bad time to visit.

You can buy one-day, one-park tickets, although such a short visit isn't recommended. If you do have only one day, however, select one park and enjoy it as an appetizer. It's no coincidence that Walt Disney World sells money-saving passes for four days (all theme parks) and five days (all theme parks as well as other attractions), and not for any shorter periods. An added incentive is that passes *don't* have to be used on consecutive days.

Which park should you visit first? The **Magic Kingdom** is what first comes to mind when most people think of Walt Disney World. Stroll down spick and span Main Street, USA to reach the six other 'lands': Adventureland, Frontierland, Liberty Square, Fantasyland, Mickey's Starland and Tomorrowland. The Magic Kingdom is where you are most likely to meet any Disney characters, though they do also appear in other parks.

Film fans will naturally be drawn to the newest of the parks, **Disney-MGM Studios**. It was Disney productions that inspired Beauty and the Beast and The Voyage of the Little Mermaid, but not all the attractions have Disney origins. You'll see stunts from the Indiana Jones films and ride in the Star Tours flight simulator on a

Making the Most of Your Time: an Eight-Point Plan

1. Make a choice of rides and attractions for each park. Look at the (free) park maps to work out a route.
2. It will save time if you buy tickets (or four- or five-day passes) in advance at Walt Disney World hotels or travel agents.
3. If you can, arrive early at the entrance, before the gates open (see p.24). That way, you'll use your ticket to the full.
4. Look at the Entertainment Schedule leaflet to check the times of parades and special events.
5. Have lunch early, or late, to avoid the midday rush.
6. Leave any shopping until after the rides.
7. Visit indoor and sit-down shows in the early afternoon – you'll appreciate the shade and air-conditioning.
8. Leave time for relaxation, especially if you have small children. You may want to take a siesta at your hotel (remember to get your hand stamped to allow you to re-enter).

giddy trip inspired by George Lucas' film *Star Wars*. Backstage, you can see both film and television production in progress, and look over the shoulders of artists working on new animated feature films.

The **EPCOT Center** will appeal more to (and is aimed at) older children and adults. EPCOT set out to be more serious than its magical neighbour, but then the *Imagineers* couldn't resist the temptation to add a lot more fun – and who's complaining? The huge park comprises two areas, Future World and World Showcase. The first highlights the worlds of energy, health, travel, communications, the land, the seas and the imagination, while World Showcase presents the culture, products and cuisines of 11 countries. Brilliant replicas of local and famous architecture are home to rides, 360° Circle-Vision films and restaurants.

For other Disney attractions see Typhoon Lagoon (p.58), River Country (p.59), Discovery Island (p.60) and Pleasure **20** Island (p.108).

The Magic Kingdom

If you're staying at one of the resorts on the monorail system, that is the quickest way to go. If your Disney accommodation is not on the monorail, you can take one of the Walt Disney World buses. If you drive yourself, you'll be directed to the vast car-park. Guests at a Disney property have free parking if they show their hotel ID card, and others should keep their parking ticket: it's valid all day.

Note where you leave your car – rows are numbered but the spaces are not, and areas are named. If you think there's a danger you'll forget whether you're in Grumpy, Sleepy or Dopey, write down the details!

Walk if you are close to the **Transportation and Ticket Center** (TTC), or take one of the tractor-hauled road trains. At the TTC, you can buy a one-day ticket for the Magic Kingdom or a four- or five-day multi-park pass. To get to the park from the car-park you can choose between a 600-passenger two-decker ferryboat or a smooth monorail train: either way will take no more than a few minutes.

MAIN STREET, USA

Beyond the tracks and station of the Walt Disney World Railroad, the scene opens out into **Town Square**, an idealized version of a small American town centre from the year 1900. It buzzes with action the whole day, with bands playing and Disney characters greeting guests and signing autographs.

Across the square on the east side (on your right as you come in), the 23-minute presentation of *The Walt Disney Story* is screened, narrated by Walt himself using excerpts from 75 hours of interviews he gave over a period of 25 years. In the foyer there's a display of historic photos and letters from famous friends and admirers, as well as some of the awards he received. You'll exit from the film show through the **Disneyana Collectibles** shop, which stocks commemorative

*O*n a hi-tech ride, one thing you can be sure of is that the unexpected is bound to happen.

plates, original hand-painted 'cels' (the celluloid drawing sheets used in the original animated films) and limited-edition reproductions.

You can also make reservations here for the very popular Diamond Horseshoe Jamboree Wild West-style floor show in Frontierland (see p.26). If you **21**

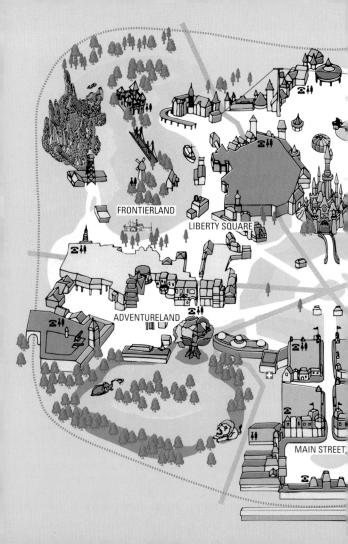

FRONTIERLAND

LIBERTY SQUARE

ADVENTURELAND

MAIN STREET

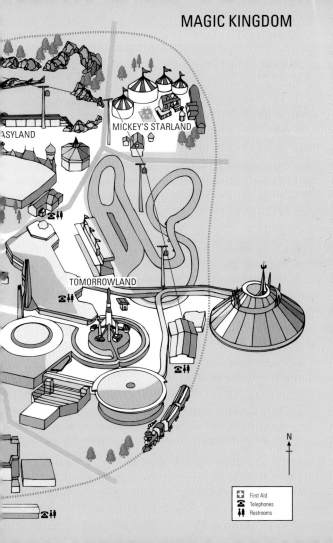

MAGIC KINGDOM

ASYLAND

MICKEY'S STARLAND

TOMORROWLAND

N

First Aid
Telephones
Restrooms

plan to go, it is advisable to sign up early.

Along Main Street

You can board a horsedrawn trolley, horseless carriage, omnibus or fire engine to ride down Main Street to Cinderella Castle, or you might prefer to stroll along, checking out the shops and a couple of attractions from bygone days. On the right, the **Main Street Cinema** presents continuous comic classics, including the historic *Steamboat Willie* (see p.13), the film that was Mickey Mouse's first hit and which also marked Minnie Mouse's debut. Although it did have a soundtrack, it is silent here because six films are shown at once, on screens all round the

---

On Your Marks...

If you've ever seen the start of the London or Boston Marathon, you'll have an idea of what '**rope-drop**' is like, except that many of those runners are all dressed the same, whereas the Magic Kingdom's early birds are the most variegated, colourful crowd imaginable.

At the end of Main Street they assemble during the hour between main gate opening and the 'official' opening, held back from their goals by a simple rope across the road. Nobody pushes. What is it about Walt Disney World that makes everyone so well-behaved?

At 9am sharp, the two cast members in charge open a gap in the middle and move the rope aside. (They used to drop it, but there was a risk of people tripping.) A wedge of assorted humanity, led by the most agile, heads through like a flying arrow, before splitting into left, centre and right-hand streams. The leftists are making for Frontierland. The centre party goes for the passage through Cinderella Castle on the way to the attractions of Fantasyland, and the charge of the right brigade is bound for Space Mountain.

room. For this same reason, you have to stand.

Across the street and down the little alley, you can get an old-fashioned shave or a haircut at **Harmony Barber Shop**. As often as not, a barbershop quartet is on hand to keep you entertained with romantic melodies. **Main Street Book Store** has the biggest collection of cards, books on the cinema and a host of children's books based on Disney films. Close by, you'll see – not to mention hear – **Penny Arcade**. Technology ranging over the last hundred years provides fun for, yes, a penny (one cent), a nickel, dime or quarter. You won't *win* any money, though. Older memories will recall some of the pinball games, even if the young who've cut their teeth on the latest electronics view them as weird relics.

The circular **Plaza**, ringed by water, is the heart of the Magic Kingdom, with bridges and walkways to its different lands leading off like spokes of a wheel. On busy days, even if you've missed rope-drop (see opposite), you could still try to beat the rush by heading for the most popular rides first: Space Mountain in Tomorrowland (see p.35), or Big Thunder and Splash Mountain in Frontierland (p.28). Tiny children might do well to escort parents to Dumbo the Flying Elephant (see p.30).

You may have formulated a plan for your journey. Here we have chosen to go clockwise, starting with a sharp left turn to Adventureland.

ADVENTURELAND

The **Swiss Family Treehouse**, doubtless the biggest you've ever seen, is built in amongst the branches of a banyan that's almost a one-tree forest. Wood would have been too much of a fire risk, so it's made of concrete and the leaves are synthetic. You climb up winding stairways through the home of the famous shipwrecked Robinson family, seeing how they lived after the disaster. (The classic novel *The Swiss Family Robinson* was the subject of a live-action Disney film.)

In **Jungle Cruise**, the vegetation is real enough and some of it needs tender loving care to keep it warm and moist, even with the Florida summer. The lions roar and the giraffes, hippos and bathing elephants look pretty convincing as your riverboat runs the gauntlet of all the imagined dangers of the darkest Amazon rainforest and assorted hostile natives.

Geography goes haywire as you travel through the African plains and glimpse a Cambodian temple, while the captain keeps up a continuous jokey commentary. Across the way, in **Tropical Serenade**, the Enchanted Tiki Birds, housed under a Balinese-looking pagoda, are some of the earliest products of Disney's *Audio-Animatronics* technology.

Perennially popular, the **Pirates of the Caribbean** get up to all kinds of skullduggery in a raid on an island fort, from the opening bombardment to a most drunken climax. Your ship sails through it all as the battle rages, and smaller children could well be frightened **26** by some of the (quite realistic) scenes of pillage, slaughter and mayhem. The way the buccaneers treat their women captives is hardly correct, either. Prepare to be shocked!

Your adventures have just begun. A short stroll takes you back to the front of Cinderella Castle, from where you can follow the way left along a little street of shops and snack bars, and turn left again. There is also a useful short-cut, down the little alley right opposite the Swiss Family Treehouse. Either way, you'll arrive in the old Wild West.

FRONTIERLAND

The frontier is of course that of the American Wild West during the 19th century, when pioneers panned for gold or drove their cattle across the range. The cast dresses for the part, in kerchiefs and denim, bonnets and gingham, while the architecture runs the full gamut from log cabin to fancy façade. Even the vegetation is vetted for authenticity.

Several times a day, the **Diamond Horseshoe Jamboree**

Parades

Daily in the **Magic Kingdom**, the carnival-style **afternoon parade** (usually at 3pm), with 5-storey Disney characters, makes its way along Main Street, through Liberty Square and Frontierland. Most evenings (at 8 or 9pm in summer with an extra show at 11pm on special nights) the **SpectroMagic** electrical parade follows the same route. It's alight with fibre-optic and laser effects, huge holographic images and a blaze of colour, tempting photographers to try and do it justice. The Plaza, the hub of the Magic Kingdom, is one popular spot for watching. Another is Town Square – especially the Walt Disney World Railroad Station and steps – which is better if you plan to leave the park right after the parade goes by.

The best viewing places tend to be grabbed early, but securing them would be hardly worth the use of your precious time on a short visit. A small fortune in **fireworks** goes up in smoke at 10pm on those summer evenings when the Magic Kingdom is open late.

always seems to have a full house. Its 30 minutes of song, dance and comedy are certainly delivered with unflagging verve by a terrific cast. You'll need tickets in advance, which are best arranged early in the morning from the hospitality desk by the Disneyana Collectibles shop on Town Square (see p.21).

At the explosive **Frontierland Shootin' Arcade** there are neither bullets nor pellets,

but infra-red beams fired by converted hunting rifles. Otherwise, you might be in Tombstone, Arizona in Wyatt Earp's day. Hits trigger off hilarious effects and the sound system provides appropriate screaming ricochets and howlin' coyotes. To stop you hogging the action, there's a 25 cent charge for each 'play'.

Along the same side of the street, in **Country Bear Jamboree** (or Vacation Hoedown), **27**

Audio-Animatronic characters perform a hilarious 15-minute stage show for country music fans – and if you're not, you'll enjoy more than a suspicion that the bears are really sending it up.

Two of the highest hills in Florida are to be found here in the Magic Kingdom, where once there was only the flattest swamp. On **Splash Mountain** your boat slowly and inexorably climbs the watery slopes, winding up your anticipation. Scenes along the way come from *Song of the South*, the part-live, part-animated movie with Brer Rabbit and Brer Fox. You pass through tunnels, twists and turns before emerging over five storeys up, where you'll hang in space before racing headlong down the 45-degree slope (which feels like a vertical drop) into the briar-fringed pool below. You'll definitely get wet, so cover your cameras and vertigo sufferers abstain! Take note of the string of boarding restrictions – for example, nobody who suffers from back or neck problems should take the ride.

The same restrictions apply on **Big Thunder Mountain Railroad**, although it's funny rather than frightening. There are no falls as precipitate as those on Splash Mountain and certainly nothing as violent as on Space Mountain (see p.35), although the safety bars that come down over your laps are not just there for decoration.

Genuine mining equipment from days gone by litters the hillside and (not so genuine) dinosaur bones stick out from the slopes where you climb on board a 'runaway' mine train which chugs to the top of the hill before rushing down at breakneck speed round unlikely bends, before regaining the safety of the station.

You reach **Tom Sawyer Island** by raft. In complete contrast to the rest of the Magic Kingdom, more adventurous children can run around here on their own, firing the guns of Fort Sam Clemens, crossing swaying bridges and exploring the caves and interesting secret passages. This can be a time-consuming expedition though, and is perhaps best kept for a second visit. Note that Tom Sawyer Island closes at dusk.

LIBERTY SQUARE

Just across the way from the wooden shacks of the Wild West, you'll have spotted a more elegant building, unmistakeably of the Colonial era. The **Hall of Presidents** brings to life *every* American president from George Washington onwards. Each of them takes a bow on stage as they're introduced, but if you glance at the others while the roll-call is going on, you'll see them turn and chat among themselves. Their movements are remarkably lifelike – more so than their faces, judging by the recent presidents. First there's a five-screen, upbeat history of the US Constitution (with the best seats at the back). Schedule the 25-minute show for a time when you feel like sitting down out of the sun.

Contrasting vessels ply the **Rivers of America**, but it's sensible to choose just one – whichever of them has a shorter delay. As a rule, that will be the *Liberty Square Stern Wheeler*, recalling the heyday of the stylish paddle steamer. The alternative trip is on one of the **Mike Fink Keelboats**, named after an early American captain. Both take you past much the same forest scenery, animals and occasional events on the river banks in a delightful gentle experience.

Stars in their eyes – 'Can I have your autograph please?'

As a contrast, you could give yourself a real fright in the **Haunted Mansion** where, count them if you can, 999 ghosts emerge from the dark grinning and jumping. It's all very good-humoured, but still not for the very small or very nervous. You'll have time to try and puzzle out how some of the special effects actually work – for example the haunted ballroom scene where several ghostly couples whirl in an eternal waltz. The answer? Holography. The journey finishes with the ghosts playing a trick so clever that it would be a shame to spoil the surprise.

FANTASYLAND

Walt Disney's dream was to make fairy stories come to life and, in those terms, this land is really the heart of the Magic Kingdom. The toytown buildings are straight out of Disney's classic films.

Several times a day (see the free Entertainment Schedule) an energetic musical show hits the **Castle Forecourt Stage** at the edge of the Plaza. Many of the songs are Disney hits, and Disney characters join in with the dancing.

Don't expect any thrilling rides inside **Cinderella Castle** itself, but spare a moment to inspect the fine mosaics which depict the fairytale, taken from scenes from the famous 1950 Disney film. Even if you don't eat there, walk up the ceremonial staircase to King Stefan's Banquet Hall. To make it a landmark, the castle was built to over 180ft (55m), more than double the height of its predecessor, Sleeping Beauty Castle in Disneyland, which almost disappeared as trees grew up around it.

Through the archway and straight ahead, the most traditional ride in the Kingdom, **Cinderella's Golden Carrousel**, is a merry-go-round of 90 galloping horses. Take a careful look: this is a genuine old fairground ride, meticulously restored and adapted. Next to it, under the cable-cars of the Skyway, duplicates of **Dumbo the Flying Elephant** circle and soar: riders have control of the height. Dumbo's manager,

Timothy Mouse, directs operations from the top of a ball in the centre. This ride is a hit with the very young and, even though it is not a long trip, limited capacity means long waits at peak periods.

On the left through the castle archway, you might miss the cinema presenting **Magic Journeys**, a 3-D film which is viewed through polarizing glasses. The realism is remarkable and it's hard not to duck as various objects fly towards you. Speaking of ducks, Donald co-stars with the special effects in the part-live, part-animated action.

Left again and round the corner you'll find yourself at the entrance to **Peter Pan's Flight**. Inspired by J M Barrie's book and the Disney film of 1953, the ride takes you in tiny flying galleons from London to Neverneverland, where the wicked Captain Hook is up to no good.

A silver and gold pavilion is home to the charming **It's a Small World**, 'the happiest cruise that ever sailed'. Everyone smiles at the hundreds of singing, dancing dolls dressed in folk costumes from every corner of the globe. Their insistent little tune will go round in your head for days! The ride is always in demand, but as upwards of 30 boats run at any one time, the lines move relatively quickly.

In the Fantasyland **Lagoon**, Captain Nemo takes you in his submarine *Nautilus* in the **20,000 Leagues Under The Sea** adventure. If you've read the book, or seen the Disney live-action film, you'll remember the attack of the giant squid, and Nemo playing the organ. If there's a long waiting time (and the queue does move slowly) come back after dark, when the special effects – artificial reefs, polar ice, and the lost city of Atlantis – are even more striking.

Snow White and the Seven Dwarfs was Disney's first full-length animated feature film, and when it was released some of it was considered to be too frightening for very small children. The same might be true of the ride **Snow White's Adventures** in which your wagon **31** rolls through the dark forest as the Wicked Witch tries to way-lay you in between attempts to catch Snow White.

The last two rides in Fanta-syland are at the far end, past the boarding point for the sub-marines. The reckless Mr Toad stole a car, so the story goes in *The Wind in the Willows*, and drove it on a mad journey through the English country-side. **Mr Toad's Wild Ride** gives you the chance to join him in a blend of ghost train and the Keystone Cops, dicing with disaster at every turn. The very young and nervous might be scared.

In the giant, whirling tea-cups of the **Mad Tea Party** you at least have some control: you can make them spin faster or slower. The idea originated from the Disney animated film of 1951, not directly from the Lewis Carroll book *Alice in Wonderland*. The ride itself is a variation on the Whip, an old fairground favourite and, like the Dumbo the Flying Ele-phant ride (see p.30), is only designed for small numbers of **32** people at one time.

MICKEY'S STARLAND

When the ageless Mouse sur-prisingly reached a 60th birth-day in 1988, the first all-new land to be added to the Magic Kingdom was opened to com-memorate the event.

Unlike the others, it doesn't start at the central hub of the Plaza. The little cartoon town of **Duckburg** is tucked away between Fantasyland and To-morrowland – you might miss it if you don't go looking for

Double Take

You don't have to be a fan of Mickey Mouse, but in Mickey's Starland it helps, because there he is, sign-ing autographs and posing with guests. He sure gets around; one minute greet-ing arrivals, the next cook-ing breakfast in a restaur-ant, only to turn up later in Town Square.

It's no good asking him how he does it – he never speaks, except in his films (when Walt Disney himself lent him his voice).

it. One sure way to get there is by taking the Walt Disney World Railroad from Town Square or from the Frontierland Station.

Mickey's House, with his car parked in front, is set up like a museum of his career. Walk through and out the back door, across the yard and into a circus-type tent where Disney videos are shown to entertain while you wait. Soon, you are invited to a still bigger tent for the live music and comedy of the **Starland Show**.

A whole cast of characters turns up from television's *The Disney Afternoon*, including Launchpad McQuack, Darkwing Duck and Chip and Dale, as well as Scrooge McDuck from *Disney's Duck Tales*.

The way out of the show is through a big souvenir shop which leads to **Mickey's Hollywood Theater**, where the Mouse himself is backstage in his dressing room. Naturally only small numbers can go in at one time, but as always, you can ask a host or hostess how long the wait will be and act accordingly.

Across the main street in Duckburg, **Grandma Duck's Farm** is alive – really alive – with chicks, goats, piglets and Minnie Moo, the cow with the extraordinary marking on her side in the shape of Mickey Mouse's head, complete with

In the theme park world of make-believe, you can become anyone or anything you want.

the famous ears. The Wisconsin farmer who bred Minnie Moo sent a photograph of her to the Disney organization – and you'll see why they just had to buy her. The farm buildings are home to a few young animals – children may pat them through the fences – and the whole operation is looked after by young farmers who'll be glad to answer questions.

TOMORROWLAND

This is the end of our clockwise journey through the other lands of the Magic Kingdom, a simple turn to the right if you've walked straight down Main Street.

Tomorrowland has one star attraction for those who are fearless, Space Mountain, and a mixture of rides appealing to various ages. Young children enjoy driving the cars of the **Grand Prix Raceway** round the twisting track. With an accelerator and brake, they have control of speed up to a modest maximum, but rails keep them mostly on one line – the steering wheel is redundant.

Compared with the newest rides, **Mission to Mars** is dismissed by fans of newer simulation as 'old technology' – which is rather a paradox since humans haven't reached Mars. You'll see what they mean, but this one still gives an odd sensation of being blasted into space by ingeniously adjusting your seat.

In 'American Journeys', the **Circle-Vision 360** cinema encircles you entirely with pictures taken by a battery of nine cameras which were variously suspended from a helicopter flying through the Grand Canyon, put on the back of a truck through New York streets, and placed close to a space shuttle launch. Standing to watch the 20-minute film, you have to turn round to see what's happening behind you.

Dreamflight goes through the history of aviation with aircraft models up to full size, wide-screen footage of stunts, a world tour, and visions of future travel.

Soar over Magic Kingdom in a **Skyway** cable-car, or take the **WEDway PeopleMover** to tour Tomorrowland on an aptly futuristic transport system propelled by friction-free linear induction (don't ask!). The bonus for any traveller on this is the glimpse of roller-coasters inside the mysterious Space Mountain.

A prominent landmark, the **StarJets**, whirling round their rocket-shaped tower, are an intricate version of a simple fairground ride for the young, or toddlers with their parents. A revolving theatre called **Carousel of Progress** takes you along with an *Audio-Animatronics* family on an amusing tour through a century of electrical gadgetry in about 20 minutes. **Tomorrowland Theater** stages musicals – sometimes moved from the Castle Forecourt Stage (see the Entertainment Schedule).

From all over Tomorrowland you'll hear the screams of deliciously terrified riders inside **Space Mountain** as they get thrown about in pitch dark and put through head-spinning manoeuvres more akin to selection tests for astronauts. If you forced anyone to do it,

you'd be accused of torture. Don't ride if you have neck or back problems – if you're under 44in (1.10m), or pregnant, you are not allowed to. The bar that comes down over your shoulders will hold you securely, but it can't guarantee the same for your property. Despite many warnings, hats, pairs of glasses, handbags (and guidebooks) are collected beneath the mountain every day, so put yours away and hang on very tightly to cameras.

You'll hardly believe it, but the hurtling cars don't reach speeds over 28mph (45kmph). The G-forces are produced by tight bends, and disorientation by spells of darkness. Many riders admit that they close their eyes, which is a pity as some of the lighting effects are beautiful and also contribute to the sensation of speed by rushing past you in the opposite direction.

You can change your mind while you're waiting and divert to see **RYCA 1/Dream of a New World**, which offers applications of electronics including seeing yourself on TV. **35**

The EPCOT Center

Most people would guess that EPCOT is an acronym, but few could say what it stands for. Walt Disney himself conceived the idea of an 'Experimental Prototype Community of Tomorrow' with one visionary scheme comprising a huge transparent dome, sealing in a whole city of harmony and progress. Sadly, in 1966 Walt Disney's death occurred before he was able to develop the details, and the EPCOT Center which was actually built involved compromises dictated by practicalities. Early in the planning, several international pavilions, intended for a site next to the Magic Kingdom, became the centre of EPCOT's World Showcase. Then Future World took off when large US corporations became excited by the concept and signed up Exxon and AT&T (led by General Motors) as sponsors.

EPCOT has two entrances: the main one near Spaceship Earth – that's the great white 'golfball' which is visible for miles around – and International Gateway in the World Showcase, intended mainly for those guests coming in from EPCOT resorts.

If you come by Disney bus, they'll drop you near the main entrance. The Disney monorail system links EPCOT with the Magic Kingdom and its resorts by way of a change of train at the Travel and Transportation Center (TTC).

From the EPCOT resorts – the Swan, Dolphin and Yacht and Beach clubs – it's only a short walk or ride on a shuttle 'tram' to International Gateway between the pavilions of France and the United Kingdom. (To avoid arguments, the waterway that divides them is called neither the Channel nor *La Manche*.)

If you come by car, you'll be directed to a place in the huge parking area. Rows are numbered and the zones are named, but in case you forget whether you're in Communication or Imagination, write down the location. Parking is free for guests who are staying in Disney-owned accommodation. Others should keep their

EPCOT CENTER

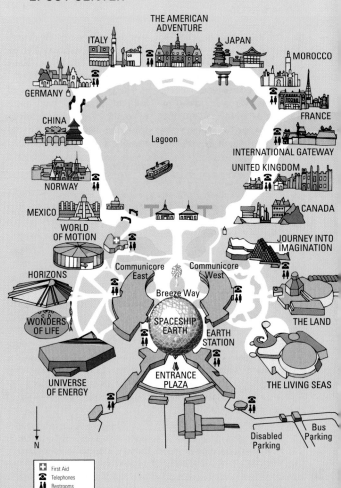

THE AMERICAN ADVENTURE

ITALY

JAPAN

MOROCCO

GERMANY

FRANCE

CHINA

INTERNATIONAL GATEWAY

Lagoon

UNITED KINGDOM

NORWAY

CANADA

MEXICO

JOURNEY INTO IMAGINATION

WORLD OF MOTION

Communicore East

Communicore West

HORIZONS

Breeze Way

THE LAND

WONDERS OF LIFE

SPACESHIP EARTH

EARTH STATION

UNIVERSE OF ENERGY

THE LIVING SEAS

ENTRANCE PLAZA

Disabled Parking

Bus Parking

N

First Aid
Telephones
Restrooms

parking ticket as it is valid for the whole day.

You'll need to buy a one-day ticket or a four- or five-day pass. Pushchairs and wheelchairs can be rented, and if in doubt, take into account the long distances you will have to walk to see both of the EPCOT worlds: jokers say the letters really stand for 'Every Person Comes Out Tired', or 'Each Parent Carries Out a Toddler'.

The park is in the shape of a figure eight, aligned north to south. Taking your bearings from the sun, the main entrance is at the north end.

A Few Tips

- Dress is ultra-casual, but visitors must not go barefoot or bare-chested in the theme parks.

- Despite the clever layout, you'll be doing quite a lot of walking and standing, so wear your most comfortable clothing, especially shoes, and watch out for sunburn.

- Guests may not bring their own food and drink into the theme parks. There are plenty of places to eat inside.

- Most attractions forbid the use of flash photography.

- If you want to leave and return (even just to go to your car), be sure to have your hand stamped at the exit. You'll need your ticket as well.

- Carry some cash for fast food and drinks. Only sit-down restaurants accept credit cards.

- Smoking is not allowed anywhere in the attractions, or in the queues or waiting areas. Restaurants have smoking and non-smoking sections.

- If you hire a pushchair (stroller), tie a bright piece of clothing to it, or when you leave it someone may take it by mistake. Then you'll have an ethical dilemma – whether to take someone else's! Keep the receipt: it's valid all day.

FUTURE WORLD

This half of the figure eight illustrates the wonders of science and communications, and the achievements of technology, both now and with predictions for the future. In recent years changes here have begun to reflect greater awareness of environmental concerns. The human dimension is also more in evidence, with an increased emphasis on biology and medicine, health and exercise.

Landmark of Future World, **Spaceship Earth** is a 180ft (55m) 'geosphere' made up of over 14,000 aluminium and plastic triangles. The 'skin' is designed so that any rainwater falling on it is funnelled inside and piped away to the lake. The ride is one of EPCOT's most popular and, uniquely, the queue starts to form before 9am because the area is accessible about 30 minutes earlier. Queues tend to be long all day, this being the first attraction that most people see. You may want to wait until evening.

The **Spaceship Earth Ride** spirals upwards, tracking the history of human communication from cave drawings and Egyptian hieroglyphics to the invention of printing. On it climbs to the advent of film, radio, television and satellite, then through an awe-inspiring 'star field' and distant views of our home planet before making a backwards descent. Near the sphere's supporting pillars, **Earth Station** is the main information and restaurant reservation centre.

The twin curved **CommuniCore** buildings flank Spaceship Earth with a circular plaza between them. As the demonstrations and interactive exhibits involve a minimal wait, or none, enjoy some of the rides before paying a visit.

On the left as you face away from the entrance, **CommuniCore East** offers Backstage Magic, a short history of computers and what they can do today, including the way they help to run the Vacation Kingdom, from hotel reservations to the *Audio-Animatronics* figures. Hosted by operator Julie and graphic helper 'I/O' (Input-Output) you will see into **39**

EPCOT's big computer centre, with holographic and other images superimposed.

At **Electronic Forum** you can cast your vote for the 'Person of the Century' – on a computer terminal, naturally – by choosing anyone you want from a list of nominees ranging from national leaders to pop stars. If you don't like the options on offer, write in your own candidate. The votes will be added up at midnight on 31 December 1999.

Exxon's **Energy Exchange** compares the output of sources ranging from pedalling a bicycle to a hydro-electric power station and answers questions. Displays look at energy options old and new: the tides and waves, wind, biomass, nuclear and hydrocarbons.

American Express' **Travel Port** gives you some ideas for your next vacation, and the huge **Centorium shop** boasts the EPCOT's biggest range of souvenirs, Disney T-shirts and other clothing.

CommuniCore West houses AT&T's **FutureCom**, displaying both today's and some of tomorrow's communication systems, with hands-on exhibits and games. At **Expo Robotics**, witness how delicately robots balance spinning tops, or have your picture sketched by a robot 'artist'. A robot will airbrush a design to your order on your T-shirt, and Kodak's **Image Magic** can print an EPCOT postcard with you set in your chosen spot.

Also in CommuniCore West is the **Outreach** and **Teachers' Center** who are ready to advise on almost any subject. If they don't have the answers, they know a computer database which does.

The Pavilions of Future World

Each in its own different and appropriate building, the seven pavilions form a circle round CommuniCore, with gaps on the north (the main entrance) and the south (where the two worlds of EPCOT join).

To get to the first pavilion you should cut through Communicore East and keep going to the left.

40

Universe of Energy: Exxon's Universe of Energy experience lasts about 45 minutes, starting with a multi-image show projected on a strange 'rotating mosaic' of screens. Moving on to the next room you watch a short animated film on the origin of fossil fuels in the days of the dinosaurs. Suddenly, in one of the best *coups de théâtre* that even Walt Disney World can boast, the seating area divides into separate cars which move off on an odyssey which takes you from the earth's creation out of whirling gas clouds right up to the 21st century. Along the way, you'll pass through primeval landscapes with dinosaurs battling and an erupting volcano. Finally, at the Energy Information Center, another film on a huge wrap-around screen conveys the impact of energy on the 20th century. The sequence of a space shuttle launch almost propels you into orbit.

Wonders of Life: In the Met Life Corporation gold-domed building, Wonders of Life focusses on biology and health.

In **Body Wars**, you are 'miniaturized' to the size of a blood cell and propelled on a reckless ride through the human cardio-vascular system to fight a bacterial infection. As in the equally popular Star Tours trip at Disney-MGM Studios (see p.54), you're strapped into a flight simulator and facing a screen where the pictures are synchronized with the cabin's movements. As in Star Tours, it doesn't all go smoothly and boarding restrictions apply.

Cranium Command takes a hilarious look at how a 12-year-old boy's mind and body learn to work together through a hyperactive day, harangued by a military martinet called 'General Knowledge'. Celebrities act the parts of the left and right sides of the boy's brain, heart, stomach and adrenal gland.

The Making of Me explores all the wonders of pregnancy and birth by combining romance, cartoon spermatozoa competing to reach the egg, and remarkable live film of a developing foetus. It's sensitively done and the warning **41**

'Please use discretion in deciding whether you or your family should view' seems to be unnecessary.

Goofy About Health has Disney's cartoon character appearing on seven screens to demonstrate the dos and don'ts of healthy living. In live shows staged throughout the day, the witty and quick-thinking **Ana-Comical Players** improvise skits involving the audience.

At the **Met Lifestyle Revue** you punch details into a computer and check on your own health habits. **Coach's Corner** gives you a chance to demonstrate your swing at golf, your tennis stroke or baseball skills, and videos and analyses your game. Or try out **Wondercycles**, exercise machines with a programmed video tour and read-outs of your speed and the number of calories you've used – which turns out to be remarkably few.

Last but not least, **Sensory Funhouse** takes the old fairground idea of distorting mirrors and extends it to all the senses, with hands-on (as well as eyes- and ears-on) exhibits.

Horizons: The whole of the Horizons building is taken up by one of EPCOT's most complex rides. On a trip through the future imagined by visionary writers and film-makers of the past, we find that most of their predictions look comical to us now. But wait a moment, doesn't that mean that *our* predictions are likely to be just as far off target? Undeterred, we laugh at Jules Verne's hero being fired to the moon from a supergun, and on through electrifying images of today's world in micro- and macro-photography, projected on a giant OmniSphere screen. Finally push a button to choose which landscape – desert, underwater or space – you want to speed through in order to end the journey.

World of Motion: This building, appropriately shaped like a wheel, takes you on a not-too-serious ride. **It's Fun to be Free!** is a 14-minute mixture of the history of real and imaginary transport ranging from cave-dwellers to Viking ships, via boneshaker bicycles, stage coaches and a great train robbery. The scenes all feature a large cast of *Audio-Animatronics* figures, and much of the old hardware is the genuine article. The automobile plays a key role with General Motors presenting a look at tomorrow's cities, with the hope that they won't be as choked with traffic as they are today.

In **Transcenter**, you can sit in a whole range of the sponsors' shiny cars, both current and 'concept'. The message that the good old internal combustion engine is still the way forward is reinforced here in a screen debate.

Odyssey Complex: Next to World of Motion, the Odyssey Complex houses the First Aid and Baby Care Center, and a Lost Children desk. Here, you have reached the crossover of EPCOT's figure-of-eight layout. You can make a detour

This business of fun and adventure is something that needs to be taken quite seriously.

into World Showcase, on foot or in one of the boats that cross the lagoon, but in this guide we continue round the circle of Future World. If you want to do the same, cut through CommuniCore West, or take the walkway by the lagoon.

Journey into Imagination: Kodak's Journey into Imagination, in its blue glass double pyramid, suggests that almost anything is possible as you take a 14-minute ride through

World Records

- The cast of 34,000 have a working wardrobe of some 2.5 *million* pieces.

- The 400 laundry operators deal with 60 tonnes of washing every day, and 32,000 garments for dry cleaning.

- Over 1,000 cleaners (known here as 'custodial hosts and hostesses') keep this world tidy. Every spot in every attraction is cleaned every night.

- Walt Disney World gardeners have planted 1 million trees, and 20 million flowering annuals.

- Well over 1 million pairs of sunglasses have been lost and never claimed.

- Guests take over 200,000 rides a day on Disney buses, monorails, boats and trams.

- The shops have sold over 34 million T-shirts, so far.

a world of wild ideas. **Magic Eye Theater** shows the 3-D movie *Captain EO*, a musical space adventure with superstar Michael Jackson. Produced by George Lucas in a *Star Wars* style, it's loud and frightening enough to give some smaller children nightmares. The 3-D effects are sensational, bringing the action to within inches of your face, and you'll see people reaching out to touch. Upstairs, **The Image Works** is **44** a 'playground of the future',

with interactive games, light and sound trickery and hands-on video screens. Not surprisingly, there's a **Cameras and Film** shop, near the Magic Eye Theater. Outside the *Caption EO* show take a look at the fascinating 'jumping' fountains, where the water jumps all by itself from one pool to another.

The Land: This pavilion (by Kraft General Foods) actually grows some of the food used in the park's own restaurants, such as the hot, red peppers in Mexico's San Angel Inn. **Listen to The Land**, a boat trip, cruises through greenhouses set up to simulate tropical rainforest, desert and the American plains, and past a traditional farmstead, looking at the world's important crops.

If you are especially interested in the above, take the 45-minute **Greenhouse Tour** instead – you walk through the same areas and learn about them in more detail. Numbers are limited, however, so make reservations early at the podium, through the gift shop near Farmer's Market food court. Starting every half-hour, the walk is guided by one of the farmers ('professional agricultural staff' in Disney parlance) who explains some of the techniques. The future of agriculture may or may not include the widespread use of hydroponics, but fish-farming is already a massive industry.

Harvest Theater shows a big-screen 70mm film, *Symbiosis*, depicting the relationship between the land and the human race. Illustrated by sev-

eral frightening examples of pollution, it also raises spirits with some upbeat stories of recovery. In **Kitchen Kabaret**, Bonnie Appetit and the Kitchen Krackpots star in an *Audio-Animatronics* song-and-dance salute to good nutrition. **Broccoli & Co** sells seeds, some of the plants grown here, and kitchen items.

The Living Seas: Housed in a building shaped rather like an octopus, United Technologies Corporation sponsors this experience, which claims to have the biggest saltwater fish-tank in the world – over 5 million (US) gallons. Next to an imitation coral reef live 80 species of tropical fish, sharks, dolphins and Florida's manatee.

You zigzag past a history of underwater exploration to board a brief ride through a submerged transparent tunnel. Then you can take as long as you like at the dual-level **Sea Base Alpha**, watching the fish and sea mammals close-up, as well as divers working in the tank. Experiments taking place are explained by the scientists, **45** and you can even try on a diving suit. At the **Coral Reef Restaurant**, you can sit and face the reef itself.

WORLD SHOWCASE

The second 'circle' of Epcot, around the shores of a lagoon, celebrates the culture and cuisine of 11 varied nations (with more participants to come). Each 'country' is housed in a microcosm of its own striking architecture, and naturally sets out to sell itself with the best possible image. In this guide we take a clockwise tour.

Mexico: An ancient Mayan pyramid looks as if it might eventually suffer the fate of its original brethren in Yucatán and be overgrown by jungle greenery. All is cool, dark and mysterious inside, with beautiful displays of priceless pre-Colombian treasures.

At the back of the building, a boat trip on *El Rio del Tiempo* (the River of Time) meanders past an erupting volcano, a film of an Aztec ceremony, an animated fiesta and market-stall traders which are all convincing enough to have you making an offer. Another film proclaiming the tourist attractions of Mexico is followed by an ingenious fibre-optic 'firework display'.

Norway: Oslo's 14th-century Akershus Castle, a turf-roofed cottage, a traditional wooden stave church, and 17th-century harbourside houses from Bergen inspired the buildings for the Norway pavilion.

Don't miss **Maelstrom**, the popular and thrilling Viking longboat voyage which takes a trip through Norway's myths and legends, meeting along the way threatening three-headed trolls and then sliding backwards down a cataract to the churning water of a North Sea storm. You disembark in a little port and see *The Spirit of Norway*, an inspirational short film that will make you want to go there. A display entitled 'To the Ends of the Earth' is housed inside, showing some relics of Nansen's and Amundsen's famous expeditions to both North and South poles.

China: Another fine collection of replica buildings centres on Beijing's circular Temple of Heaven, the perfect setting for showing a Circle Vision 360° film travelogue, the *Wonders of China*.

Along the Great Wall and down the Yangtze River, and from Lhasa to Shanghai, you will see more of China in just 19 minutes than a visit could cover in a whole year. You'll need eyes in the back of your head to see it all, of course, and having to stand may be tiring for some.

You won't be able to take your eyes off the shows and characters in fairytale theme parks.

Germany: Food and rural cosiness is the scene in the German pavilion, where the main attraction is the **Biergarten**, with plenty of German food and loud, rousing music. For all the folksy image, the little toytown-like shops are engaged in real business: chocolates at **Süssigkeiten**, wines in the

47

Weinkeller, and **Volkskunst** for those crafts and souvenirs that everyone takes home from Germany, from beer steins to cuckoo clocks.

Italy: Beautifully detailed replicas of the Doge's Palace and the Campanile recreate a miniature of St Mark's Square in Venice, complete with gondola moored at the lakeside. Other buildings, statues and gardens round the piazza are based on originals from various regions of Italy. A troupe of strolling comic actors and singers often pulls a crowd and talks some of them into performing, with predictably dire results.

The United States: You won't be surprised to find the host nation taking centre spot at the head of EPCOT's lagoon. Presented by two potent US corporations, American Express and Coca Cola, two centuries of American history pass painlessly by in no more than half an hour in *The American Adventure* (a name often given to the whole pavilion). It uses some of the most advanced

Audio-Animatronic figures yet made, headed by hosts Mark Twain and Benjamin Franklin.

Japan: The well-groomed gardens with their waterfalls, little bridges and carved stone lanterns make a perfect retreat from the somewhat distracting world around. The tall, stepped pagoda and 'flying roof' palace are based on historic temples of Nara and Kyoto. As well as four restaurants, the pavilion houses the **Bijutsu-kan Gallery** of traditional and contemporary art.

Morocco: As the only representative here of the Arab and Islamic worlds, Morocco took its responsibility very seriously. Moroccan workers were sent to construct perhaps the most authentic of all the World Showcase buildings. The superb tilework and intricate detail are not so much replicas as a living art-form – look out especially for the **Fez House** and fountain. The **Gallery of Arts and History** displays art treasures, intricate embroidery and jewellery, and in a re-creation of an ancient kasbah, artisans work with brass and silver.

France: Not surprisingly, gastronomy is the main theme here, and three superstar chefs (Bocuse, Lenôtre and Vergé) are advisors to the restaurants. The big, five-screen 18-minute travelogue *Impressions de France* will also whet your appetite for a trip. If you think you know the country already, think again!

You'll hardly mistake the mini-Eiffel Tower for the real thing, but the rest of the architecture is a *real tour de force* in 19th-century Parisian style. From mansard roofs through pavement cafés and down to the banks of a waterway a little like the Seine, it catches the atmosphere better than by trying to be an exact replica.

International Gateway: As EPCOT opened, it made sense to give quicker access to the park. 'Trams' run to and from the Swan and Dolphin, and Yacht and Beach Clubs, but the walk along the waterfront path only takes a few minutes.

The United Kingdom: Somehow designers have managed to compress a composite English village-town-city, with a dash of Scotland and Wales too, into a living travel brochure. Architectural styles ranging from early Tudor to high Victorian are included, in convincing detail.

The **Rose & Crown** pub feels quite like home to British visitors – and the beers are quite authentic (but cold and pasteurized to suit American tastes and laws).

Canada: Inspired by the Château Laurier in Ottawa, Hôtel du Canada is the landmark. Massive though it looks, even close-up it's really not much bigger than a good-size house.

O Canada! is a Circle-Vision 360° film that takes you from coast to coast through the great outdoors. You'll wish you had 360° eyes too, as the pictures taken by a nine-camera battery from helicopters, planes, sleds and canoes surround you. So does the sound, most sensationally in the ice-hockey match.

49

Disney-MGM Studios Theme Park

Celebrating the American love affair with movies, the newest of the big three at Walt Disney World opened in 1989. Probably more like 1930 Hollywood than Hollywood ever was, its art-deco streets lead you along to real and replica sets. They really do make film and television programmes here, as you'll see through the windows into the working studio areas. There's plenty of audience participation, for all ages, in the attractions and street 'happenings'.

If you come by car, signs are easy to follow from the I-4 or US192 highways. Parking is free for guests at Disney-owned accommodation, if they show their resort ID card. Others should keep their parking ticket – it's valid all day – and remember where you park. If you are staying at one of the EPCOT resorts, you can come **50** by waterbus. Check when the park closes: this varies from 7pm onwards.

TOURING DISNEY-MGM

Once through the gates, you may feel like you're in a California dream, but even if there is an impromptu show going on in the street, don't linger. Similarly, you can check out shops and buy a snack later. Instead, walk straight ahead down **Hollywood Boulevard** towards **Sunset Plaza**. On the right you'll see a huge board chalked with the latest information on times of shows and special events.

In this guide, we follow a route which roughly circles the park in a clockwise direction, but you'll need to be flexible. If you want to ride Star Tours (see p.54), you'd do well to go straight there at opening time, and then make for the Indiana Jones Stunt Spectacular (see p.53) for the first session of the day. After that, you might get quickly into the queue for one of the behind-the-scenes tours (see p.54). By the time you come out, the queues will have

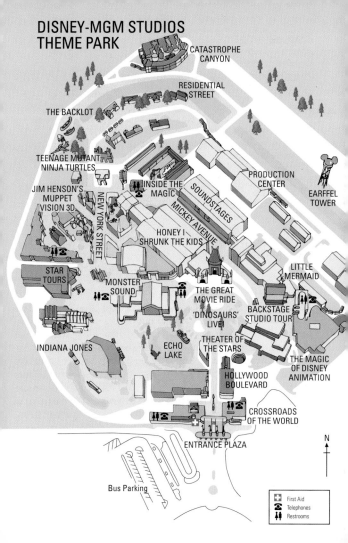

DISNEY-MGM STUDIOS
THEME PARK

CATASTROPHE
CANYON

RESIDENTIAL
STREET

THE BACKLOT

TEENAGE MUTANT
NINJA TURTLES

PRODUCTION
CENTER

INSIDE THE
MAGIC

SOUNDSTAGES

EARFFEL
TOWER

JIM HENSON'S
MUPPET
VISION 3D

NEW YORK STREET

MICKEY AVENUE

HONEY I
SHRUNK THE KIDS

STAR
TOURS

LITTLE
MERMAID

MONSTER
SOUND

THE GREAT
MOVIE RIDE

BACKSTAGE
STUDIO TOUR

'DINOSAURS'
LIVE!

INDIANA JONES

ECHO
LAKE

THEATER OF
THE STARS

THE MAGIC
OF DISNEY
ANIMATION

HOLLYWOOD
BOULEVARD

CROSSROADS
OF THE WORLD

ENTRANCE PLAZA

N

Bus Parking

First Aid
Telephones
Restrooms

All The World's a Stage

It was a stroke of genius to call the people who work at Walt Disney World, all 34,000 of them, 'cast members'. This is the entertainment business, the reasoning goes, and just as certain rules apply to the acting profession, so they do here. The language reflects this: the cast wear 'costumes', not uniforms, and they're kept in the 'wardrobe', not the locker room. When they're in view of the visitors (the 'guests'), they're 'on stage' – and there's no smoking or drinking.

Actors and actresses would never wear the wrong sort of jewellery or make-up: nor do the Disney cast. No eyeliner or very bright lipstick for the women, no large earrings, a maximum of one ring per hand, and no 'facial hair' for men (except for the *Imagineers* and animators: after all, Walt himself had a moustache).

built up at all the popular attractions, but at least you'll have had a head start.

Check the schedule of the nearby **Theater of the Stars** for the times of the live stage musical based on Walt Disney Pictures' animated hit, *Beauty and the Beast*. You can see some of it without waiting for a seat, if you're pressed for time. Make a note of the times of another show not far away on Sunset Plaza. Based on another Disney animated feature, it brings to life the story of the

Voyage of the Little Mermaid in a delightful musical production – the song *Under the Sea* won the film an Oscar. Combining live performance and puppets as well as film clips, it takes place in an undersea grotto with a curtain of water and other special effects. Realism extends to spraying the audience gently and filling the theatre with bubbles, so cover your camera.

Meanwhile, in the middle of Sunset Plaza, the **Star Today** (a major or minor name from films or TV) will turn up periodically – details are given in the Entertainment Schedule.

THE RIDES

The **Chinese pagoda** on Sunset Plaza is a full-size replica of **Hollywood's Chinese Theater**, where stars' foot- and handprints are set in cement – here they've done the same. Inside, the 20-minute **Great Movie Ride** is a tribute to some of the landmark productions of a hundred years of film-making. Your *seat* moves on a twisting track through vivid scenes from *Casablanca*, *The Wizard of Oz*, *Raiders of the Lost Ark* and dozens more classics, with life-size *Audio-Animatronics* figures of stars and some realistic special effects (perhaps too realistic for very small children). This is one of the most popular attractions and queues grow soon after the park opens.

While you wait to get into the **Monster Sound Show**, you'll see a video of an old Disney expert, the late Jimmy McDonald, who not only invented thousands of tricks to simulate sounds, but also took over as Mickey Mouse's voice when Walt Disney gave up the position in 1946. In the show itself, people from the audience help to add the sound effects to a scene of insurance salesman Chevy Chase arriving at a haunted house, with hilarious results.

SuperStar Television is a live re-creation of the making of some of TV's all-time hit shows such as *I Love Lucy*, *The Golden Girls* and *General Hospital*, with some of the audience taking part. Clever cutting makes the final footage feature them interacting with the real stars, past and present.

Check the schedules and go quickly to the vast open-air theatre for the **Indiana Jones Stunt Spectacular**, which occurs several times a day. Generally you need to get there in advance of the start times. It's live, of course, on three sets that move (you don't have to), and you can even join in – if you dare. 'Extras' are chosen from the audience before the show, so be there early if you **53** want to volunteer. Some sequences reveal 'how it was done' in *Raiders of the Lost Ark* and *Indiana Jones and the Temple of Doom*, and in a specially devised climax the scene explodes in sheets of flame.

 At **Star Tours**, a battered 'Starspeeder' space-craft with *Star Wars* characters C3P0 and R2D2, as well as deranged robots at work, suggests that all might not be as smooth as the space travel agency claims. On board, you're welcomed by a loony captain with a head like an upturned wok ('Your first trip? Mine too!'). Then the thrills begin as you experience the 'virtual reality' of a runaway ride. The flight simulator cabin is thrown around while graphic scenes of the hazards of flying through a comet's tail, an interstellar dog-fight, or along the streets of a hostile city are perfectly synchronized on the big screen in front of you. It's not for the very nervous – and there's a string of other warnings and boarding restrictions.

Jim Henson's **Muppet*Vision 3-D** sends flying objects right at you and surrounds you with special effects, fibre optics and *Audio-Animatronics* figures of Muppet characters as well as 'live' ones. Keep an eye, if you can, on the walls of the elaborate new theatre towards the end of the 15-minute show for a surprise.

Did you see the film ***Honey, I Shrunk the Kids***, in which a careless scientist accidentally miniaturizes his and the neighbours' children down to the size of ants? Here you'll discover what it might be like to roam through a forest of 25ft (7.5m) blades of grass and meet insects as big as a house. Small children can clamber up 'spiders' webs' and slide down tubes of foliage or a huge roll of discarded 'film'.

BEHIND-THE-SCENES TOURS

Try to go early in the day to **The Magic of Disney Animation**, because there probably won't be a long wait, and you are more likely to see artists at work early in the day rather than at lunchtime or in the late

54

afternoon. The starting point is just off Sunset Plaza behind Theater of the Stars, and much of it is a self-guided walk, beginning with a short and hilarious film, *Back to Never Land*, a lesson in the basics of animation. With Walter Cronkite as the host and Robin Williams not quite ready to be animated, you will learn how a roughly sketched cartoon character is given life.

Next comes a real animation studio where you can take your time to move along, looking through the windows and over the shoulders of artists. You'll see each department – not all at work at any particular moment, but video-monitors along the way will explain – developing the story, drawing the characters to convey movement and emotion, designing the special effects and backgrounds, carefully hand-painting the plastic 'cels' (see p.21) and photographing them one-by-one.

Last comes the editing, and as a finale you'll see special

Creating the Magic

'Don't they mind being watched?' Everyone on the **Magic of Disney Animation Tour** wants to know how the artists feel, working under the gaze of thousands of visitors each day. The answer is apparently 'yes and no'. Loss of privacy is balanced by the fact that they are being acknowledged instead of hidden in a back room. Now there's no doubt the balance has succeeded: the 70 artists here created 15,000 drawings and eight months' work for both *Beauty and the Beast* and *Aladdin*.

'Have there been any advances in technique since Walt Disney's day?' Disney would recognize everything going on here, though the artists have a written script now, whereas Disney kept the story in his head. Changes are on the way, however, with the possibility of 'paperless animation', modelling in 3-D on computer screens. The artists are ready: 'It will allow us to be even more creative.'

Which Did You Miss?

It may save a lot of arguments, or start them, but here's a list of all the Walt Disney animated feature films.

1930s

Snow White and the Seven Dwarfs (1937)

1940s

Pinocchio (1940); *Fantasia* (1940); *Dumbo* (1941); *Bambi* (1942); *Saludos Amigos* (1943); *The Three Caballeros* (1945); *Make Mine Music* (1946); *Fun and Fancy Free* (1947); *Melody Time* (1948); *The Adventures of Ichabod and Mr Toad* (1949)

1950s

Cinderella (1950); *Alice in Wonderland* (1951); *Peter Pan* (1953); *Lady and the Tramp* (1955); *Sleeping Beauty* (1959)

1960s

One Hundred and One Dalmatians (1961); *Sword in the Stone* (1963); *The Jungle Book* (1967)

1970s

The Aristocats (1970); *Robin Hood* (1973); *The Many Adventures of Winnie the Pooh* (1977); *The Rescuers* (1977)

1980s

The Fox and the Hound (1981); *The Black Cauldron* (1985); *The Great Mouse Detective* (1986); *Oliver and Company* (1988); *The Little Mermaid* (1989)

1990s

The Rescuers Down Under (1990); *Beauty and the Beast* (1991); *Aladdin* (1992)

Where does *Mary Poppins* fit in? Answer: it was one of Disney's mixtures of live action and animation, like *Song of the South*. This list includes only pure animation.

sequences from famous films including *Bambi* (Walt Disney once admitted it was his favourite), *101 Dalmatians* and *Cinderella* in the Disney Classic Theater.

The best examples of the animator's art have now come to be recognized as modern classics and connoisseurs pay high prices for them. Original 'cels' (see p.21) once sold for a few dollars each, but they can now fetch several thousand dollars. In the **Animation Gallery** here you'll see examples on sale.

The afternoon is probably a good time to go on the excellent **Backstage Studio Tour**, beginning near the Little Mermaid show off Sunset Plaza. Departures are almost continuous for the 20-minute shuttle ride, taking you first through costuming and scene building, then past stored props and old cars, and even old aircraft. **Residential Street** is an outdoor set with some backless 'houses' that may look familiar from films and TV shows (*The Golden Girls'* house, for example). Then, watch out! In **Catastrophe Canyon** you get a memorable close-up 'by accident' of the artificial floods, fires and explosions that gave disaster movies their name. If you're sitting on the right side, you may get splashed, and on the left you definitely will, so cover your camera. Incidentally, it only takes 3½ minutes to recycle the 70,000 gallons (318,000 litres) of water and to have the catastrophic chain of events ready for a replay.

You can break off the tour at this stage, but if you're ready to go on, follow Roger Rabbit's pink, painted footsteps to **Inside the Magic: Special Effects and Production Tour**, a walking tour which takes from 45 minutes to an hour to complete. To start with, you'll see how hurricanes and sea battles are simulated in a tank, with a member of the audience as the hapless captain in one storm-tossed model. Then a couple of children are asked to play the miniaturized kids who take a flight on a bee in *Honey, I Shrunk the Kids*, while you learn some optical and mechanical secrets. Next you look **57** down into three real working sets: Soundstages I-III. Check the Entertainment Schedule to see what may be going on, and which star personalities might be around.

In **Post-Production Editing and Audio**, the editors and sound engineers explain how they add the finishing touches. The tour finishes in the Walt Disney Theater with previews of Disney and Touchstone productions coming, in the time-honoured phrase, 'to a theater near you'.

The restaurants in Disney-MGM Studios are part of the show. **The Hollywood Brown Derby Grill**, near Theater of the Stars, has a Wall of Fame of caricatures, and talkalikes of the two famous gossip-column queens, Louella Parsons and Hedda Hopper, might well be at one of the tables. At **50's Prime Time Café** you can eat while vintage sitcoms play on television. The **Sci-Fi Drive-In Diner** serves up sandwiches while you sit in booths like 1950s convertibles and watch science-fiction B-movies from **58** the same period.

Other Walt Disney World Attractions

(Note that during bad weather some of the waterparks such as Typhoon Lagoon and Wet 'n' Wild (see p.86) may close.)

TYPHOON LAGOON

Faced with the competition of other waterparks round Orlando, Disney responded with this one with parking that is free to Walt Disney World Resort guests. Towels can be hired, and unusually for Walt Disney World parks, you can take in your own food and drink (no alcohol or glass) though food is available at two restaurants.

The park is imaginatively landscaped: in this 56-acre (22ha) South Sea island setting you can forget you're miles inland: there's even a white sand beach for basking, and plenty of trees for shade.

The main attraction is the giant **wave generator** which sends perfect bodysurfing rollers up to 6ft (1.8m) in height across the 2.5-acre (1ha) blue lagoon, every 90 seconds. Periodically it goes into a gentler mode, producing non-breaking waves – then a horn sounds a warning before the 'big ones' start again.

Mount Mayday, rising 90ft (27m) above the lagoon, has the wreck of a shrimp boat, the *Miss Tilly*, perched convincingly on its peak as if cast there by a passing tidal wave. Climb up the hill for the view, shielding your camera from the frequent waterspouts that erupt from *Miss Tilly*'s funnel.

From over 50ft (15m) up the slope, a couple of giant water slides – **Humunga Kowabunga** – send you screaming at 30mph (50kmph) through a tunnel to plummet into the lagoon. It's not for very small children, and there are a number of other restrictions. You may like to work up to it by first trying one of the shorter slides which twist their way in and out of caves and waterfalls on the way to splashdown.

For a gentler ride you can hop on the rubber inner tubes through the white water cascades of **Mayday Falls** and **Keelhaul Falls**, or go four at a time down **Gangplank Falls**. If the queues have grown too long, pick up an inner tube at one of the collection points and let **Castaway Creek** float you gently along, circling the park and meandering through woods and grottoes.

Free equipment is available for snorkelling over **Shark Reef**, an artificial coral reef but with shoals of *real* fish and even some small (and harmless!) sharks as companions.

For the very young, **Ketchakiddie Creek** has paddling pools, small slides and fountains. If you forgot to bring swimwear, **Singapore Sal's** has a good selection, as well as sun protection cream, hats and every other beach essential.

RIVER COUNTRY

On Bay Lake near the Magic Kingdom, this is a longer-established waterpark than Typhoon Lagoon. It has fewer and smaller slides and no wave machine, but many people like **59** its relaxed atmosphere. Towel rental is available.

Instead of a tropical theme, River Country is designed as a rustic 'ol' swimmin' hole'. The thrills come from **Whoop 'n' Holler Hollow**, two long corkscrew waterslides which rush you out of the trees to splash into the giant pool. Or ride an inner tube down the **White Water Rapids**, stretch out on the sandy beach and picnic at the tables (you can bring your own food and drink in, but no alcohol or glass).

DISCOVERY ISLAND

A little world of its own exists almost unnoticed in the middle of Walt Disney World, and few visitors ever find it. On this 11-acre (4ha) island in **Bay Lake**, you can roam almost at will amid hosts of real birds and animals. Fifty species of wild bird are regularly logged, with 100 more in aviaries.

Trails and boardwalks wind their way through the cunningly contrived landscape and the lush greenery. Along the way, you'll spot swans, ringtail lemurs, peacocks, golden lion tamarins and giant Galapagos tortoises. Many of the animals move around freely, though you are subtly separated from the alligators and crocodiles, and all the inhabitants feel so unthreatened by visitors that you can get very close.

This is an accredited zoological park, with a growing record of success in breeding endangered species of bird. It specializes in hornbills, and was the second zoo in North America to raise the rare rhinoceros hornbill.

On arrival, take note of the time of the next **Bird Show**. In a humorous performance, several talking macaws show off.

Discovery Island is reached by boat from River Country, Fort Wilderness, the Contemporary Resort, and from the Magic Kingdom near the main entrance.

PLEASURE ISLAND

This resort primarily provides entertainment in the form of nightclubs and discos and is covered in detail on p.108.

Other Attractions in the Orlando Area

✓ UNIVERSAL STUDIOS FLORIDA

More than just a theme park, **Universal Studios Florida** is billed as the 'biggest film and TV production facility east of Hollywood'. Your feet will believe it after a whole day here, which you'll need to experience some thrilling rides and see a selection of shows.

North of International Drive and signposted off the I-4 interstate highway, it's easy to find by car. As with all theme parks, make a note where you leave your car.

Our suggestions on making the most of your time on p.19 generally apply here as well: try to arrive before the 9am opening hour, collect a guide

leaflet and map at the gate, decide your priorities, and make your way quickly to one of the popular attractions to beat the rush. Towards the end of each day people take up positions for the evening **Spectacular**, an explosive show set on the lagoon with high-speed boat chases and plenty of firepower.

The park is divided into six areas – on the map at least. On the ground the distinction does not much matter. This guide

*Y*ou may well tell yourself it's only a plastic model, but you still can't help screaming.

takes them here in a roughly clockwise order, but the route you choose may be different as you head for your objectives. **The Front Lot**, near the main entrance, includes most of the administrative clutter of Guest Relations desk, bank, lockers, pushchair and wheelchair rental, lost children and property, and production information –

what's happening in the studios or on the sets.

Production Central

Straight ahead down **Plaza of the Stars** and right where it starts at the crossroads is one of the big attractions of Production Central, the **Funtastic World of Hanna-Barbera**.

*E*ven laser-generated spooks don't have a ghost of a chance against Ghostbusters in Universal Studios' show.

The partnership of Bill Hanna and Joe Barbera created the ever-popular cartoon characters of the *Flintstones*, *Yogi Bear* and *Scooby Doo* – you may see the characters outside greeting the fans. This ride is a flight simulator which takes you on a thrilling high-speed chase, driven by Yogi Bear, who obviously hasn't yet passed his test. It's not as violent as some rides of this kind, and stationary seats are provided at the front for the very young or anyone who would prefer not be rocked around.

The **Production Tour** tram chugs past sets that may be familar from television shows – take it if you need to sit down. The late king of suspense presents a bag of tricks in **Alfred Hitchcock's 3-D Theatre**, where (and even more arresting in this format) *The Birds* or the *Psycho* shower come straight at you. In the shop you can buy Bates Motel hand towels for your favourite guests. In *Murder She Wrote* **Mystery Theatre**, the audience moves from one stage to another of a frantic production

---

Dilemma!

Which should you choose, Universal Studios Florida or Disney-MGM Studios? Once they were both open, comparisons became inevitable.

Universal Studios is a lot bigger (which doesn't just mean more of the same), and there isn't the cosy, fairytale feeling of the Disney-MGM Studios., Also, fewer of the attractions are based on films made for the youngest audiences. In addition, the streets and sets of Universal Studios are on a grander scale, so there's more walking, but it does have some of the most thrilling rides you'll experience anywhere, though they might scare small children.

Of course, true film fanatics will want to head for both Disney-MGM *and* Universal.

process and 'helps' to put together a scene.

Hollywood

Hollywood, off to the right, is a 1950s street set in chrome and pastel. Among the shops and cafés selling Hollywood hats, sunglasses and posters, the attraction – if you can call it that – is the **Gory Gruesome and Grotesque Horror Make-Up Show**. The name says it all.

New York

It's easy enough to find New York, straight ahead from the main entrance, with its replica Manhattan sky-scrapers. The *Ghostbusters* show piles on the special effects: slime, ectoplasm, lasers and other high technology. Don't expect it to make sense!

Meanwhile, out in the street, two Blues Brothers lookalikes pull up in their battered ex-cop car and do song and dance routines from the movie of the same name. In **Kongfronta-**

64 **tion**, mighty King Kong, four

storeys high, has escaped and is rampaging through the city, swatting helicopters like flies. You are riding in a cable-car high above the street (don't ask why!) when Kong attacks. Your life hangs by a thread ... It's one of the biggest attractions in every way. Watch out for a time when the waiting line isn't too long, but don't miss it. You can also check out your reaction in a video playback afterwards.

San Francisco/Amity

Clustered round one end of the lagoon, San Francisco/Amity features sets of Fisherman's Wharf and Amity (*Jaws*) Harbour, snacks and seafood and two outstanding attractions.

Earthquake – The Big One puts you in a San Francisco subway train, standing quietly at a station, when the quake begins. The roof falls in, chasms open in the platform, a truck from the street above slides down straight at you and a tidal wave rolls in. The effects have been calculated at 8.3 on the Richter scale.

A Selection of Hotels and Restaurants in Walt Disney World and Orlando

Recommended Hotels

The Orlando area, including Walt Disney World, has more hotel rooms than anywhere else in the United States. Fierce competition in the highly developed hospitality industry means that you'll be assured of value for money, whether you choose the most luxurious resort, a modest motel or something between the two.

Here we offer a selection of hotels in each price range, listed in alphabetical order, with telephone numbers, and fax numbers where possible. Location may be important, depending on whether you intend to spend most of your time in Disney territory, to visit other attractions or to travel more widely in central Florida. We have therefore sub-divided the list by area, and marked each entry with a symbol indicating the price range, per night, for a double room with bath, excluding breakfast. Taxes of about 10% are added to hotel bills.

In the US, rates are quoted for the room, not per person. If you have more than two occupants, you may be charged a small supplement. Some hotels include a simple continental breakfast. Always ask about special rate packages, eg for stays of a few days.

⦀⦀	above $180
⦀⦀	$100-$180
⦀⦀	$60-$100
⦀	below $60

WITHIN WALT DISNEY WORLD

Guests staying in Disney accommodation may use Disney transportation and sports facilities, and have privileges when making reservations for shows etc. Car parking at the theme parks is free for them, and entry to the parks by Disney transportation is guaranteed, even when they are 'full' to others. These advantages compensate for the higher prices of rooms within Walt Disney World.

All-Star Resorts ⦀⦀⦀

Walt Disney World, Lake Buena Vista, Florida FL32830
Tel. (407) 939-5000 (sports)
Fax (407) 827-8655
Tel. (407) 939-6000 (music)
Fax (407) 939-78222

Sports and music themed resort. Disney's most inexpensive accommodation. 1,900 rooms.

Caribbean Beach Resort ‖

Walt Disney World, Lake Buena Vista, Florida FL32830
Tel. (407) 934-3400
Fax (407) 934-3288
Near the EPCOT Center. Colourful and pretty 'village' design around a lake disguises its huge size. Themed pool and marina. 2,112 rooms.

Contemporary Resort ‖‖‖‖

Walt Disney World, Lake Buena Vista, Florida FL32830
Tel. (407) 824-1000
Fax (407) 824-3539
A fifteen-storey 'vaulting horse' shape, next to Magic Kingdom. Monorail service passes through the huge lobby. Floor show, pools, marina. 1,053 rooms.

Dixie Landings Resort ‖

Walt Disney World, Lake Buena Vista, Florida FL32830
Tel. (407) 934-5800
Fax (407) 934-5777
Not far from the EPCOT Center, and very convenient for all areas of Walt Disney World. The 'Old South' theme of plantation homes and wooded setting conceals its

enormity. Pools and a waterway and 2,048 rooms.

Grand Floridian Beach Resort ‖‖‖‖

Walt Disney World, Lake Buena Vista, Florida FL32830
Tel. (407) 824-3000
Fax (407) 824-3186
The Grand Floridian offers the marvellous re-creation of Victorian splendour. Monorail service to Magic Kingdom. Pools, marina, beach. 901 rooms.

Polynesian Resort ‖‖‖‖

Walt Disney World, Lake Buena Vista, Florida FL32830
Tel. (407) 824-2000
Fax (407) 824-3174
'South Sea Island' longhouses are set next to the Seven Seas Lagoon. Outside is the monorail service to Magic Kingdom. Pools, beach. 855 rooms.

Port Orleans Resort ‖

Walt Disney World, Lake Buena Vista, Florida FL32830
Tel. (407) 934-5000
Fax (407) 934-5353
Not far from the EPCOT Center, and convenient for all areas, this hotel is set in the 'French quarter' of the New Orleans themed area. Themed pool area and waterfront. 1,008 rooms.

67

Walt Disney ||||
World Dolphin

Operated by Sheraton Hotels,
PO Box 22653, Lake Buena
Vista, Florida FL32830-2653
Tel. (407) 934-4000.
Fax (407) 934-4099.

A short walk to the EPCOT Center's International Gateway. It's a vast tower in salmon and green. Marina, pools. 1,510 rooms.

Walt Disney ||||
World Swan

Operated by Westin Hotels,
PO Box 22786, Lake Buena
Vista, Florida FL32830-2786
Tel. (407) 934-3000
Fax (407) 934-4499

A short walk to the EPCOT Center's International Gateway. Arc-roof tower topped by swans. Marina, pools, beach. 758 rooms.

Yacht Club & ||||
Beach Club Resorts

Walt Disney World, Lake Buena
Vista, Florida FL32830
Tel. (407) 934-7000 (Yacht Club)
(407) 934-8000 (Beach Club)
Fax (407) 934-3450

A short walk to the EPCOT Center's International Gateway. Twin re-creations of majestic 19th-century Massachusetts coast resort. Marina, themed pools and a beach. 1214 rooms.

DISNEY VILLAGE
PLAZA HOTELS

Designated 'Official Hotels of Walt Disney World', these are inside Walt Disney World but are not Disney-owned. Entry to the theme parks by Disney bus is guaranteed, and guests may play golf and tennis at Disney Village.

Buena Vista Palace |||

1900 Buena Vista Drive, Lake
Buena Vista, Florida FL32830
Tel. (407) 827-2727
Fax (407) 827-6034

A lakeside tower complex and convention centre. Tennis, pools, gardens. 841 rooms.

Grosvenor Resort |||

1850 Hotel Plaza Boulevard,
Lake Buena Vista, Florida
FL32830
Tel. (407) 828-4444
Fax (407) 828-8120

Tower block with convention facilities. Tennis, pools. 630 rooms.

Hilton |||

1751 Hotel Plaza Boulevard,
Lake Buena Vista, Florida
FL32830
Tel. (407) 827-4000
Fax (407) 827-6380

Huge C-shaped block with a convention centre. Garden, pools, tennis and restaurants. 813 rooms.

Howard Johnson   III
Resort Hotel
1805 Hotel Plaza Boulevard,
Lake Buena Vista, Florida
FL32830
Tel. (407) 828-8888
Fax (407) 827-4623
14-storey tower and lower annexe.
Pools, garden and family-oriented
dining. 323 rooms.

Royal Plaza   III
1905 Hotel Plaza Boulevard,
Lake Buena Vista, Florida
FL32830
Tel. (407) 828-2828
Fax (407) 827-6338
17-storey block and wings. Ten-
nis, pool, garden. 396 rooms.

Travelodge Hotel   III
2000 Hotel Plaza Boulevard,
Lake Buena Vista, Florida
FL32830
Tel. (407) 828-2424
Fax (407) 828-8933
18-storey tower. Pool and garden.
325 rooms.

CLOSE TO WALT DISNEY WORLD/KISSIMMEE

Comfort Inn   I-II
8442 Palm Parkway, Lake Buena
Vista, Florida FL32819
Tel. (407) 239-7300
Fax (407) 239-7740

A large budget hotel with the
ubiquitous pools. 640 rooms.

Days Inn East of   II
Magic Kingdom
5820 West Irlo Bronson
Memorial Hwy. (US192),
Kissimmee, Florida FL34746
Tel. (407) 396-1000
Fax (407) 396-1789
Budget hotel. Pools. 604 rooms.

Gala Vista Motor Inn   I
5995 West Irlo Bronson
Memorial Hwy. (US192),
Kissimmee, Florida FL34746
Tel. (407) 396-4300
Motel with good size rooms, pool.
200 rooms.

Holiday Inn   II
Maingate East
5678 West Irlo Bronson Memorial
Hwy. (US192), Kissimmee,
Florida FL34746
Tel. (407) 396-4488
Fax (407) 396-8915
Large and family-oriented hotel.
Pools and children's entertain-
ment. 670 rooms.

Hyatt Regency   III-IIII
Grand Cypress Resort
1 Grand Cypress Boulevard,
Orlando, Florida FL32836
Tel. (407) 239-1234
Fax (407) 239-3800

69

A spacious resort and convention centre with golf courses, tennis courts, pools, a lake, sailing, equestrian centre and delightful large gardens. 750 rooms.

Larson's Lodge   I
Maingate
6075 West Irlo Bronson
Memorial Hwy. (US192),
Kissimmee, Florida FL34747
Tel. (407) 396-6100
Budget hotel but, of course, with pools. 128 rooms.

Marriotts Orlando   IIII
World Center
8701 World Center Drive,
Orlando, Florida FL32821
Tel. (407) 239-4200
Fax (407) 238-8757
A towering resort hotel complete with a convention centre, golf course, tennis courts, pools, many restaurants and splendid large gardens. 1,500 rooms.

Orange Lake   II
Country Club
8505 West Irlo Bronson
Memorial Hwy. (US192),
Kissimmee, FL34746
Tel. (407) 239-0000
Fax (407) 239-5119
Rooms, apartments and villas all in a resort complex. Tennis courts, pools, a golf course, and plenty

of watersports on the lake. 362 rooms/villas.

fuality Inn   I- II
Maingate
7675 West Irlo Bronson
Memorial Hwy. (US192),
Kissimmee, Florida FL34747
Tel. (407) 396-4000
Fax (407) 396-0714
Economy hotel, pool. 200 rooms.

Radisson Inn   III
Lake Buena Vista
8686 Palm Parkway, Lake
Buena Vista, Florida FL32836
Tel. (407) 239-8400
Large rooms, pools, and gardens. 200 rooms.

Ramada Resort   II
Maingate
2900 Parkway Boulevard,
Kissimmee, Florida FL34747
Tel. (407) 396-7000
Large resort in spacious grounds. Pools, tennis. 400 rooms.

Sheraton Lakeside   II
7769 West Irlo Bronson
Memorial Hwy. (US192),
Kissimmee, Florida FL34747
Tel. (407) 396-2222
Fax (407) 239-2650
Lakeside resort, family-oriented. Pools, tennis, large gardens, mini-golf. 651 rooms.

ORLANDO: INTERNATIONAL DRIVE AREA

Delta Orlando $II

5715 Major Boulevard, Orlando, Florida FL32819
Tel. (407) 351-3340
Fax (407) 351-5117
A family-oriented budget resort. Pools, garden, tennis, mini-golf. 800 rooms.

Gateway Inn $II

7050 Kirkman Road, Orlando, Florida FL32819
Tel. (407) 351-2000
Fax (407) 363-9366
Family-oriented economy hotel. Pools. 354 rooms.

Heritage Inn $II

9861 International Drive, Orlando, Florida FL32819
Tel. (407) 352-0008
Fax (407) 352-5449
Charming hotel with pool. 670 rooms, each with verandah.

Howard Johnson $II

5905 International Drive, Orlando, FL32819
Tel. (407) 351-2100
Fax (407) 252-2991
An economical 21-storey round tower hotel with swimming pools and a sauna. 302 rooms.

Peabody Orlando $IIII

9801 International Drive, Orlando, Florida FL32819
Tel. (407) 352-4000
Fax (407) 351-0073
A towering 27-storey landmark with a convention centre. Tennis courts and large pool. 851 rooms.

Ramada Resort Florida Center $II

7400 International Drive, Orlando, FL32819
Tel. (407) 351-4600
Fax (407) 363-0517
A bright, convenient resort hotel, with indoor and outdoor pools, tennis, and garden. 380 rooms.

Rodeway Inn International Drive $II

9956 Hawaiian Court, International Drive, Orlando, Florida FL32819
Tel. (407) 351-5100
Fax (407)352-7188
Economy hotel, low-rise buildings around pool. 222 rooms.

Sheraton World Resort $II

10100 International Drive, Orlando, Florida FL32821
Tel. (407) 352-1100
Fax (407) 352-2632
Low-rise buildings in large gardens, pools, mini-golf. 788 rooms. **71**

Sonesta Villa Resort ▮▮▮
10000 Turkey Lake Road,
Orlando, Florida FL32819.
Tel. (407) 352-8051
Fax (407) 345-5384
Villa complex in large grounds. Tennis courts, pools, golf adjoining. 369 rooms.

Stouffer Orlando Resort ▮▮▮
6677 Sea Harbor Drive,
Orlando, Florida FL32821
Tel. (407) 351-5555
Fax (407) 351-9991
Ten-storey tower and convention complex, but also suited to families. Pools, tennis. 778 rooms.

Twin Towers ▮▮▮
5780 Major Boulevard,
Orlando, Florida FL32819
Tel. (407) 351-1000
Fax (407) 363-0106
Two glass towers. Convention facilities. Pools, garden. 760 rooms.

ORLANDO: NORTH AND DOWNTOWN

Choice Inn ▮
4201 South Orange Blossom Trail, Orlando, Florida FL32809
Tel. (407) 849-6110
Small economy hotel south of downtown. Pool. 68 rooms.

Colonial Plaza Inn ▮▮
2801 East Colonial Drive,
Orlando, Florida FL32803
Tel. (407) 894-2741
Fax (407) 896-9858
Near Fashion Square. 225 rooms.

Harley of Orlando ▮▮-▮▮▮
151 East Washington Street,
Orlando, Florida FL32801
Tel. (407) 841-3220
Fax (407) 849-1839
Downtown lakeside hotel in traditional style. Pool. 305 rooms.

Holiday Inn Winter Park ▮▮
626 Lee Road, Winter Park,
Florida FL32810
Tel. (407) 645-5600
Fax (407) 740-7912
Four miles north of downtown Orlando. Pools. 202 rooms.

Omni Centroplex ▮▮▮
400 West Livingston Street,
Orlando, Florida FL32801
Tel. (407) 843-6664
Fax (407) 839-4982
Close to downtown. 300 rooms.

Radisson Plaza ▮▮▮
60 South Ivanhoe Boulevard,
Orlando, Florida FL32804
Tel. (407) 425-4455
Downtown and close to route I-4. Pools, tennis. 337 rooms.

Recommended Restaurants

Everywhere you turn, there's somewhere to eat, and almost everything is open seven days a week. Here we give a selection of full-service restaurants, buffet restaurants and food courts (multiple outlets sharing a table area); for reasons of space we cannot list even a fraction of the vast number of quick-service restaurants and all-you-can-eat buffets which are well within our lowest price range. Many of the restaurants outside the theme parks serve inexpensive lunch buffets and go over to full service in the evening.

Entries are listed in alphabetical order with a symbol indicating the price range, per person, for a 3-course meal. Drinks, gratuities and 6% sales tax are not included.

▌▌▌	$30 and over
▌▌	$15–$30
▌	up to $15

WITHIN WALT DISNEY WORLD RESORT

Akershus Restaurant ▌▌
Norway Pavilion, EPCOT
(reservations at World Key)
Norwegian buffet of cold and hot dishes, from herring and salmon to goat's cheese and desserts.

Ariel's ▌▌▌
Beach Club Resort
Tel. 934-3357
Seafood – steamed and baked lobster, clams, mussels, fresh fish.

Au Petit Café ▌▌
France Pavilion, EPCOT
(no reservations)
Pavement café under canopy with informal French cooking: salads, onion soup, coq au vin, pastries.

Biergarten Restaurant ▌▌
Germany Pavilion, EPCOT
(reservations at World Key)
Veal, smoked pork, *bratwurst* and other German specialities, with traditional entertainment by musicians, dancers and yodellers.

Bistro de Paris ▌▌▌
France Pavilion, EPCOT
(reservations at World Key)
Traditional French ambience with fine, colourful and inventive cuisine, and a menu devised by some master chefs.

73

Boatwright's   ‖

Dixie Landings Resort
Tel. (407) 934-6000
Like a riverboat under construction. American and Cajun food.

Bonfamilles   ‖

Port Orleans Resort
Tel. (407) 934-5504
In the Old French quarter of New Orleans. Creole and American: oysters, crawfish, and salads.

Cape May Café   ‖‖‖

Beach Club Resort
Tel. (407) 934-3358
A New England-style clam bake every night. Seafood buffets.

Cap'n Jack's Oyster Bar   ‖

Disney Village Marketplace
Tel. (407) 828-3900
Crab, lobster, clams and oysters, plus vegetarian and non-seafood.

Le Cellier   ‖

Canada Pavilion, EPCOT
(no reservations)
Cafeteria service of international and Canadian dishes.

Chef Mickey's Village Restaurant   ‖

Disney Village Marketplace
Tel. (407) 828-3900
Family menu of pasta, seafood and standard American fare. The 'chef' Mickey Mouse makes an appearance each evening.

Chefs de France   ‖‖‖

France Pavilion, EPCOT
(reservations at World Key)
Exceptional service and fine, innovative cuisine, including specialities devised by chefs Paul Bocuse and Roger Vergé, as well as master pastry chef, Gaston Lenôtre.

Colonel's Cotton Mill   ‖

Dixie Landings Resort
Tel. (407) 934-6000
Large food court with Cajun buffet, pizzas and pasta, grills and roasts, fast food and desserts.

Contemporary Café   ‖

Contemporary Resort
Tel. (407) 824-1000
American/international menu with prime rib of beef and salad bar. Buffet breakfasts with all the favourite Disney characters.

Coral Café   ‖

Walt Disney World Dolphin Hotel
Tel. (407) 934-4000 ext. 6160
In the Dolphin Hotel (see p.68), à la carte and theme buffet dinners.

Coral Reef Restaurant   ‖‖‖

The Living Seas Pavilion, EPCOT
(reservations at World Key)

Dramatically situated, facing the big artificial reef. The menu concentrates on seafood bisques and grills, seafood and pasta.

County Fair Restaurant ‖
Hilton at Disney Village/Plaza
Tel. (407) 827-4000 ext. 3091
Cafeteria and buffet service of American cooking, chiefly barbecued chicken and beef, salads, and desserts.

Crockett's Tavern ‖
Pioneer Hall, Fort Wilderness
Resort & Campground
Tel. (407) 824-2900
All-American steaks, chicken, salads, seafood and desserts in an informal setting.

Dolphin Fountain ‖
Walt Disney World
Dolphin Hotel
Tel. (407) 934-4000 ext. 6077
A 1950s-style 'ice-cream parlour' with burgers and fries and other fast-food staples – and ice-cream.

Empress Room ‖‖‖
Aboard Empress Lilly *riverboat,*
Disney Village Marketplace
Tel. (407) 828-3900
As elegant as anywhere in Walt Disney World. Traditional 'continental' cuisine in wine-and-cream based sauces, soufflés.

End Zone Food Court ‖
Disney's All-Star Resorts
Sports-themed arena featuring such American specialities as Pizza, pastas, sandwiches and family platters.

50s Prime Time Café ‖
Disney-MGM Studios
Theme Park
Tel. (407) 560-7729
Sit by a 50s TV playing 50s sitcoms and eat 50s favourites such as meatloaf and grilled chicken.

Fireworks Factory ‖
Pleasure Island
Tel. (407) 934-8989
Interesting variety including barbecues, smoked chicken, citrus chicken. Vegetarian and low-calorie dishes available.

Fisherman's Deck ‖
Aboard Empress Lilly *riverboat,*
Disney Village Marketplace
Tel. (407) 828-3900
Seafood is the speciality here – shrimp, scallops, and fresh fish. But there are meat and vegetarian alternatives too.

Flagler's ‖‖‖
Grand Floridian Beach Resort
Tel. (407) 824-2383
Italian and international cuisine served by singing waiters.

75

Garden Grove   ‖
Walt Disney World Swan Hotel
Tel. 934-3000 ext. 1618
Spacious greenhouse setting for buffets, American cooking. Breakfast with Disney characters.

Harry's Safari Bar and Grill   ‖
Walt Disney World Dolphin Hotel
Tel. (407) 934-4000 ext. 6155
Safari decor and fresh grilled seafood and steaks.

Hollywood Brown Derby Grill   ‖
Disney-MGM Studios
Tel. (407) 560-7729
Salads, grills and pasta in 1930s California revisited.

King Stefan's Banquet Hall   ‖
Cinderella Castle,
Magic Kingdom
Tel. (407) 824-5520
Medieval setting, but 20th-century American food.

Land Grille   ‖
The Land Pavilion, EPCOT
(reservations at World Key)
Revolving restaurant overlooking the ride at the Land Pavilion. The salads and vegetables you eat here come from the pavilion's greenhouses. Charcoal grills.

Liberty Tree Tavern   ‖
Liberty Square, Magic Kingdom
Tel. (407) 824-6461
In the style of an 18th-century inn. Cooking is American with a New England touch; oysters, chowders, pasta and chicken dishes.

L'Originale Alfredo di Roma Ristorante   ‖
Italy Pavilion, EPCOT
(reservations at World Key)
Ossobuco and pasta including the speciality – 'fettucine Alfredo'. Strolling musicians.

Mama Melrose's Ristorante Italiano   ‖
Disney-MGM Studios
Tel. (407) 560-7729
Italian-Californian cuisine – pasta, brick-oven pizza.

Marrakesh   ‖‖
Morocco Pavilion, EPCOT
(reservations at Earth Station)
Moroccan specialities: couscous, kebabs, *tagine*, served to the accompaniment of musicians and a belly-dancer.

Narcoossee's   ‖‖
Grand Floridian Beach Resort
Tel. (407) 824-2383
Lakeside setting for American cuisine in typically large measures: lobsters, steaks, sundaes.

Old Port Royale ▮▮
Caribbean Beach Resort
Tel. (407) 934-2830
Food court with six service outlets offering roasts, barbecues, Italian cuisine and desserts.

The Outback ▮▮▮
Buena Vista Palace,
Disney Village/Plaza
Tel. (407) 827-3430
Big steaks and big lobsters are the specialities in this Australian-themed restaurant.

Palio ▮▮▮
Walt Disney World Swan Hotel
Tel. (407) 934-1281
Northern Italian cooking in an elegant setting. Strolling musicians.

Pompano Grill ▮▮
Disney's Village Resort
Tel. (407) 828-3735
Country club setting with cuisine Florida-style – healthy options.

Portobello Yacht Club ▮▮
Pleasure Island
Tel. (407) 934-8888
Northern Italian and seafood specialities.

Rose & Crown ▮▮
UK Pavilion, EPCOT
(reservations at World Key)
Traditional British fare: roast beef and Yorkshire pudding, fish and chips, trifle and cheeses.

San Angel Inn ▮▮▮
Mexico Pavilion, EPCOT
(reservations at World Key)
Beside the 'River of Time' ride, serving Mexican dishes both familiar and unusual.

Sci-Fi Dine-In Theater Restaurant ▮▮
Disney-MGM Studios
Tel. (407) 560-7729
Seating is in mock-ups of 1950s convertibles, with clips from old sci-fi films. Sandwiches, salads.

Steerman's fuarters ▮▮▮
Aboard Empress Lilly *riverboat,*
Disney Village Marketplace
Tel. (407) 828-3900
Steaks and roast prime rib, as well as some non-beef alternatives.

Sum Chows ▮▮
Walt Disney World Dolphin Hotel
Tel. (407) 934-4000 ext. 6150
Unusual Chinese decor and North Chinese cuisine.

Tony's Town Square Restaurant ▮▮
Town Square, Magic Kingdom
Tel. (407) 824-6793
Italian standard fare; pasta dishes are a speciality.

77

Traders ‖
Travelodge Hotel,
Disney Village/Plaza
Tel. (407) 828-2424
Caribbean sugar plantation house setting, island seafood and steak dishes from around the world.

Trail's End Buffeteria ‖
Pioneer Hall, Fort
Wilderness Resort
Tel. (407) 824-2900
American cafeteria food, pizzas, Italian buffet Saturday nights.

Victoria & Albert's ‖‖‖
Grand Floridian Beach Resort
Tel. (407) 824-2383
Elaborate elegant and formal setting, American/continental menu.

Yachtsman Steakhouse ‖‖‖
Yacht Club Resort
Tel. (407) 934-3356
Steaks cooked over a wood-fired grill, rack of lamb.

ELSEWHERE IN THE ORLANDO AREA

B-line Diner ‖
Peabody Hotel, 9801
International Drive, Orlando
Tel. (407) 352-4000
Snacks to main meals, 24 hours a day, in chrome and glass decor, to the sound of a 50s juke box.

Bimini Bay ‖
Sea World, 7001 Sea
World Boulevard,
Tel. (407) 363-2468
From snacks and sandwiches to, of course, seafood dishes. Casual.

El Bohio ‖
5756 Dahlia Drive, Orlando
Tel. (407) 282-1723
Authentic Cuban café: beans, rice, shredded beef, fried plantain etc.

Bonanza ‖
3615 West Highway 192,
Kissimmee
Tel. (407) 396-7536
Lavish buffet with entrée order.

Bubbalou's Barbeque ‖
1471 Lee Road, Winter Park
Tel. (407) 628-1212
Southern-style barbecue spot with a casual atmosphere.

Capriccio ‖‖‖
Peabody Hotel, 9801
International Drive, Orlando
Tel. (407) 352-4000
Genuine Italian country cooking with top quality fresh ingredients.

Charley's Steak House ‖
6107 South Orange Blossom
Trail, Orlando
Tel. (407) 851-7130
Steak and seafood with a salad bar.

Charlie's Lobster House ||
Mercado Mall, 8445
International Drive, Orlando
Tel. (407) 352-6929
Everything in shells or scales, any way you like.

Cattleman's Steak House |
2948 Vineland Road, Kissimmee
Tel. (407) 397-1888
Big steaks grilled over charcoal.

Chatham's Place ||||
7575 Phillips Boulevard, Orlando
Tel. (407) 345-2992
Informally elegant dining, French-influenced and innovative cuisine.

China Coast ||
7500 International Drive,
Orlando
Tel. (407) 351-9776
Informal, mainly Cantonese food. Economical lunch buffet.

Chris's House of Beef ||||
801 John Young
Parkway, Orlando
Tel. (407) 295-1931
Traditional steakhouse with some non-beef alternatives.

Le Coq au Vin ||
4800 S Orange Avenue, Orlando
Tel. (407) 851-6980
Informal, genuinely French country cooking, bistro-style.

Darbar ||
The Marketplace, 7600 Dr
Phillips Boulevard, Orlando
Tel. (407)-345-8128
Mughal decor and mostly North Indian cooking.

Dux ||||
Peabody Hotel, 9801
International Drive, Orlando
Tel. (407) 352-4000
Elegant restaurant with innovative cuisine. No duck served, respecting the hotel's resident mascots.

Gary's Duck Inn ||
3974 South Orange Blossom
Trail, Orlando
Tel. (407) 843-0270
Despite the name, it concentrates on seafood. Informal atmosphere.

Hard Rock Café |
Universal Studios Florida, 5800
Kirkman Road, Orlando
Tel. (407) 351-7625
Burgers and sandwiches, fries and shakes, to the sound of non-stop rock records. Entry from street as well as from studios.

Jordan's Grove ||||
1300 South Orlando
Avenue, Maitland
Tel. (407) 628-0020
Inventive American cuisine in the setting of a gracious old house. **79**

Lili Marlene's ‖

Church Street Station, Orlando
Tel. (407) 422-2434
Part of the entertainment complex, in an elaborate 1890s revival setting. Standard American menu.

Maison et Jardin ‖‖

430 Wymore Road South,
Altamonte Springs
Tel. (407) 898-6634
Elegant old hillside mansion in a garden setting, like a country club. Ambitious international menu.

Ming Court ‖‖

9188 International
Drive, Orlando
Tel. (407) 351-9988
Cantonese and other regional Chinese cooking in elaborate setting.

Park Plaza Gardens ‖‖

319 South Park Avenue,
Winter Park
Tel. (407) 645-2475
Elegant garden courtyard in which to try inventive international, Caribbean and French dishes.

Pebbles ‖

12551 SR535, at Crossroads,
Lake Buena Vista
Tel. (407) 827-1111
Ideas from all over the USA (California, Key West etc) go into the menu and the decor.

Phoenician ‖

The Marketplace, 7600 Dr
Phillips Boulevard, Orlando
Tel. (407) 345-1001
Mediterranean menu. Eat all the appetizers and you'll hardly have space for a main course.

Ran-Getsu ‖

8400 International
Drive, Orlando
Tel. (407) 345-0044
Elegant setting for fine Japanese food: *sushi*, *sukiyaki*, *tempura*.

Rolando's ‖

870 Semoran Boulevard,
Casselberry
Tel. (407) 767-9677
Genuine Cuban cooking in an informal, easy-going atmosphere.

Shogun ‖

6327 International
Drive, Orlando
Tel. (407 352-1607
The American version of a Japanese steakhouse. The chefs are part of the show.

Siam Orchid ‖

7575 Republic Drive, Orlando
Tel. (407) 351-0821
The taste of Thailand: chilli, coriander, lemon grass – adapted to American palates, unless you tell them to give it to you straight.

It's quite a relief when the director shouts 'Cut!' Not the least amazing sight is the huge set reconstructing itself ready for the next cycle.

The other big event here, opened in the summer of 1993, is **'Jaws'**. Yes, he's back (believe it or not) – and he's out to get you – just when you thought it was safe to go back in the water. Head off on the boat ride that almost ends in disaster as the 32ft (10m) great white shark attacks relentlessly (with a bit of help from sophisticated special effects and advanced technology!).

After all this computer-controlled engineering, the **Wild, Wild, Wild West Stunt Show** is an old-fashioned contrast.

*S*ongs and somersaults from the perenially popular Blues Brothers are recreated regularly in the street at Universal Studios.

It's fast and funny, with plenty of fist fights, gun fights and falling off roofs and horses.

Expo-Center

The attractions here include **Animal Actors' Stage**, where some of the secrets of training dogs, cats and birds to 'act' are revealed and the trainees are put through their paces. Of course, they don't always do what's expected.

ET's Adventure is a gentle journey on a starbike to help ET's home planet, with some nice special effects. The last word in rides, however, with the biggest queues (so some people run straight here when the main gates open in the morning) is the dynamic and thrilling **Back to the Future**, which takes flight simulator technology to new heights of realism and scale. While you are thrown about in DeLorean-shaped vehicles, the special effects and pictures are wrapped around you on monster hemispherical OmniMax screens. The story, such as it is, does **82** not really matter.

The guitar-shaped building on your plan of Universal Studios is the **Hard Rock Café**, the largest one in the world. (You can also reach it from outside the park, through the separate entrance.) If you want to re-enter the park, have your hand stamped before leaving, here or at the main gate.

SEA WORLD

Marine parks are a Florida tradition and this is the biggest and best. **Shamu**, the friendly killer whale featured on the park's logo, is the star turn, but the various other attractions here could easily entertain and painlessly educate you all day. On the other hand, if you only have 2 or 3 hours, you can zip round and still see most of the highlights.

Near the south end of International Drive, Sea World has that first essential of Orlando theme parks, its own exit signs from the I-4 highway. At the gate, you'll be given an invaluable map marked with the times of each show, specially printed out as you enter. Use it to plan your visit. The distances betwen shows are not large and the shows are cleverly scheduled so you can easily move from one to another, fitting in one or two other attractions on your way. Near the entrance, you can change any money, rent lockers, wheelchairs or pushchairs (strollers), naturally in the shape of dol-phins, and ask about any special tours.

All over the park you can feed the dolphins, sealions and seals in their feeding pools.

The Shows

At **Whale and Dolphin Stadium**, you'll see the all the sorts of tricks that started the whole

*T*he 'Back to the Future' ride takes simulation to new levels of realism by using a hemispherical, wrap-around screen.

marine park phenomenon in Florida. Dolphins dance, somersault, do formation aerobatics and shake flippers with one of the children from the audience. Beluga whales, meanwhile, show that they're just as clever and almost as agile.

Aware of the doubts some people have about the ethics of keeping and training captive animals, Sea World emphasizes its role in conservation and research and backs several kinds of 'green' causes. In the shows, the trainers go out of their way to stress the care that is taken of the cast. It's hard not to believe they're having fun, though some will always argue that they only do it for the food.

Sea Lion and Otter Stadium is the venue for another of the more old-fashioned circus-type performances. Supposedly set in prehistoric times, it's fast and fun. The animals (plus a vast, hairy walrus) trick the cavemen, and convey an environmental message by picking up litter. **Sea World Theater** screens *Window to the Sea*, a programme on underwater re-

search and sealife with some remarkable footage of Shamu giving birth to her calf, Namu, in 1989. In the same location in the late afternoon, you can see a lights and music *Water Fantasy* show.

At **Shamu Stadium**, on the far side of the big lake, the star's extended family of killer whales entertain three times a day plus a 'Night Magic' extra on certain evenings. It's the event not to miss at Sea World, and the big seating area fills up well before the start. The front 10 or 12 rows can expect to get splashed, if not completely soaked, by several hundred of the 6 million gallons of salt water in the tank, so don't sit there if you value your camera, or your hairstyle. As much as the agility and gentleness of the 4-ton whales, you'll also marvel at the skill and balance of their trainers. who get rocketed out of the water on the tip of a whale's nose.

The **Atlantis Waterski Stadium** faces the lake between Shamu Stadium and the entrance. The show, two or three times a day, is a themed acro-

batic stunt and formation 'ballet' on skis. If you've been to Cypress Gardens (see p.90), you'll know what to expect.

Other Attractions at Sea World

Some of the best things can be seen at practically any time of the day, mostly without a wait. In **Tropical Reef**, you stand in the cool darkness facing thousands of colourful fish in a huge, brilliantly lit aquarium, with separate tanks to keep incompatible species apart. Outside again, you can feed the

*S*aying hello at Sea World (top) and bombing out at Wet 'n' Wild (above).

harbour seals in their pool, and actually go and touch one of the stingrays in theirs.

On a hot and sticky Florida day you'll envy the inmates of **Penguin Encounter**, a large tank refrigerated to the Antarctic chill that penguins prefer. Five tons of snow fall every day! As you drift by on a moving walkway, the glass walls let you see the residents hilariously marching and slipping on the rocks and ice, and then zooming away underwater.

Terrors of the Deep is not particularly terrifying, in spite of being surrounded by the largest collection in the world of various species of sharks as well as venomous and deadly fish such as lionfish, eels and scorpion and puffer fish. You will be safely housed in a long, transparent 6in (15cm) thick underwater tunnel.

From underwater to high up in the sky, you can ride to the top of the needle-like 400ft (122m) **Sky Tower**, which is worth it if only for the view (there's a small charge).

Two special **tours** also cost extra. On the 90-minute long

86

Behind the Scenes Tour you can learn about the care, training, feeding and breeding of the 8,000 mammals, birds and fish who reside here, and the 45-minute **Let's Talk Training Tour** lets you see the actual 'classes' going on.

Finally, Sea World has entered the business of 'dinner-and-show', with a **Polynesian Luau** by the lake taking place in the early evening.

WET 'N' WILD

You might have supposed that there are only a certain amount of ways you can climb steps, slide down, and splash into a shallow pool. Here they have thought of all those, and then some – there are now 14 different slides and rides. Right on International Drive (at Republic Drive, exit 30A south off the I-4 highway), Wet 'n' Wild is convenient to reach from the hotels in that area.

From gentle slopes perfect for a baby, the slides range up in terror to culminate in **The Black Hole**, where you corkscrew down in total darkness, carried by a 5 tons per minute stream of water. In between, there's a loop-the-loop tubular slide, the 200ft (61m) Blue Niagara and many more.

In **Bomb Bay**, the newest attraction, opened 1993, riders climb up to a compartment shaped like a large bomb and are then manoeuvered over a six-storey waterslide. The control is entirely in the hands of the ride operator, who may well just let you sweat it out before opening the door and watching you free fall 76ft (23m) into the water below.

Lifeguards are always on hand to make sure people do not take risks, break the rules or get into difficulties. Wave machines generate regular 4ft (1.2m) rollers for body-surfing in a big pool, or for a more tranquil experience, you can meander along Lazy River on a rubber tube.

It's all a great way to cool off and take a break from the 'dry' theme parks. The obvious question is: How does Wet 'n' Wild compare with Disney's Typhoon Lagoon (see p.58)? The answer is, Wet 'n' Wild offers more slides, and some are indeed wilder, so if you're looking for pure thrills, this is the place to be. Typhoon Lagoon, on the other hand, has more beach, more shade and a bigger wave pool.

DOWNTOWN ORLANDO

In downtown Orlando, old and run-down buildings clustered around a once shabby railway station have been cleverly restored and extended to create the popular **Church Street Station**, a wonderful cluster of colourful and eclectic shops, food and entertainment outlets, arcaded streets and a real, shiny steam locomotive. It's all open – though fairly quiet – during the day, but after about 5pm the shows start up and you have to pay to go in.

The shows to choose from include a turn of the century-style saloon along with cancan dancers and New Orleans jazz, **Rosie O'Grady's Good Time Emporium**, and a diso, **Phineas Phogg's Balloon Works**. Just across the street is the **87**

Cheyenne Saloon and Opera House, a three-level extravaganza of wood panelling, brass and stained glass, a top class country band, an all-singing, all-dancing show and western food. Now that more people have come to this part of town, there's also plenty more restaurants, bars, clubs and discos.

'The train at Church Street Station ...', is staying right where it is, in downtown Orlando.

West of Church Street and across the I-4 highway, the **Performing Arts Center** puts on concerts, touring ballet and opera; the **Arena** is home to top flight professional basketball team, the Orlando Magic; and the **Citrus Bowl** is a football stadium seating 70,000.

Expensive suburbs start just north of here. At Loch Haven Park (take exit 43 off the I-4 (Princeton Street) and go east for 1 mile/1.6km), the **Orlando Museum of Art** is small but eclectic. Loan exhibitions

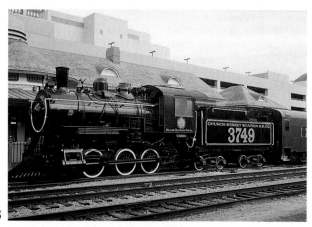

alternate American and African art, but the greatest strength is in the pre-Colombian pieces from Peru and Mexico, dating from 2000 BC to AD 1500.

Another time frame, BD (before Disney), persists in **Winter Park**, a posh district where wealthy northerners came to spend the winter as long ago as 1890. Now the millionaire mansions are joined by chic restaurants, stylish hotels and fashionable shops. The **Morse Museum of American Art** (133 East Wellbourne Avenue) is a magnet for lovers of art-nouveau glass, and home to an unrivalled collection of Tiffany lamps, vases and beautiful windows rescued from the fire which destroyed the home of Louis Tiffany (son of the jewellery maker, Charles).

KISSIMMEE

Endless ribbons of highway lined either side by billboards, motels, gas (petrol) stations, T-shirt outlets and other somewhat tacky tourist traps don't hold out much hope on the way to Kissimmee. Is there a real Kissimmee? Where's the old town that existed before all this? Not at **Old Town**, which is a modern pastiche with food outlets and specialist shops, on route US192 at No. 5770, near the I-4. It's also home of the **Elvis Presley Museum**, which claims to possess the biggest collection of Presley memorabilia outside Graceland.

You'll find traces of original Kissimmee, the little cattle town founded in 1880, along Broadway and Main Street. There's still a livestock auction each Wednesday morning (at 805 East Donegan Avenue) and a great rodeo takes place twice a year.

Giant alligator jaws herald the entrance to **Gatorland Zoo** (on route 441 near Kissimmee). The serious purpose of this place is farming the 5,000 alligators and crocodiles (animal lovers stay away) who reside here – you'll learn how to tell the difference when you get here. Since people are fascinated by reptiles, it seemed logical to turn the farm into a tourist attraction, so they have included other animals, such **89** as monkeys and other reptiles, to create a small zoo. You can ride round the park on a train and walk above the kind of swamp where alligators like to live: it covered a large part of Florida pre-theme parks and remnants remain in the Everglades. The party piece at Gatorland is feeding time. At the Gator Jumparoo (four times a day), you'll see some of the inmates 'jumping' (actually they are pushing themselves up on their tails) to catch a suspended chicken carcass. The alligators' own meat isn't wasted, and you can try out deep-fried 'gator snacks ('you've seen the show, now eat the cast'). You can also buy belts, boots, handbags and wallets made from their skins.

Aviation buffs should not miss the **Flying Tigers Warbird Air Museum** at Kissimmee Airport (North Hoagland Boulevard entrance). Workers here are geniuses at resurrecting historic aircraft to full flying condition, and the hangar is full of treasures, including a World War II Mustang, Thunderbolt and a B-25 Mitchell.

Outside, a dozen 1960s jets are waiting their turn for treatment. From the same airport, you can take a flight in the airship painted like Sea World's *Shamu* which you'll have seen circling over the theme parks. Still more thrilling, they also offer flights in old open cockpit biplanes.

Excursions from Orlando

CYPRESS GARDENS

(*Go west on the I-4 highway towards Tampa, then take the US27 exit south and follow signs to Winter Haven, then head right at Waverly and go along route 540 for about 5 miles/8km*)

An easy 40-mile (65km) drive south west from Orlando, near the old-established resort of Winter Haven, this 223-acre (90ha) lakeside park began as a botanic garden in the 1930s, which in fact makes it Orlando's oldest theme park. Now it's more famous for the spectacular **waterski shows** staged several times a day. Some of the world's champion performers do balletic lifts, acrobatic stunts and circus clown routines and form human pyramids, while microlight aircraft buzz overhead.

The noisy waterski show contrasts with the usual calm of the gorgeously manicured gardens and, a tradition here, the **southern belles** in crinoline dresses and hooped petticoats who stroll in among the flowers and sit twirling their parasols, trying not to look hot. The Kodak **Island in the Sky** is a circular platform on a mechanical arm which raises a new load of passengers 153ft (46m) every few minutes. It's worth being up there during one of the waterski shows.

They make it look so easy – the famous and impressive waterski show at Cypress Gardens south of Orlando.

Back on the ground, **Southern Crossroads** is a replica of an old Florida country town from around the year 1900, complete with shops, restaurants and collections of bygones.

Electric boats take you on waterways that wind through the gardens' different environments, from strictly formal to tropical jungle, while guides tell you about the (over) 8,000 species of plants as well as the wildlife. In spite of the efforts of the owners (Busch Entertainment Corporation) to add more attractions – for example a model railway and trapeze artists in a circus tent – there's probably not quite enough to keep you here for a whole day. (You can buy a combined ticket at a discount for the three Busch-owned properties: Sea World (see p.82), Busch Gardens (see p.97), and Cypress Gardens.)

*P*eace and tranquillity: Cypress Gardens and 'southern belle' (left) and the octagonal Bok Singing Tower (right).

BOK TOWER GARDENS

(*Continue past the Cypress Gardens exit on US27 for 5 miles (8km), exit on route 17A to Alt. US27, then turn left on Burns Avenue for about 1½ miles/2.5km*)

Florida's highest hill may be only 324ft (99m) above sea level, but it does stand out from the flat landscape near Lake Wales, south west of Orlando. It became even more of a landmark when Edward Bok, a Dutch-born New York writer

93

and publisher founded a 128-acre (52ha) nature reserve and garden here and topped it with an elegant 205ft (62m) belfry. Built of pink and grey marble carved into a blend of Gothic and art nouveau, the octagonal **Bok Singing Tower** houses a 57-bell carillon which rings a variety of gentle tunes every half-hour. They are pre-programmed, but at 3pm on most days a live carillonist plays a 45-minute recital of hymns, folk tunes and classics.

The oddly ethereal sound doesn't seem to deter the birds from singing, and the tranquil gardens and pleasant, shaded forest walks make an idyllic contrast to the nearby theme park world of concrete, plastic and excess decibels.

SPACE COAST

(*From Orlando take the Beeline Expressway east directly to Cape Canaveral*)

It's an easy 50-mile (80km) drive due east from Orlando (via a small toll) to the coast, right where America's astronauts are launched into space.

The **John F Kennedy Space Center** sent the first mission to land a man on the moon in 1969. Once home of the early NASA launches, today it is the home of the Space Shuttles – to find out when the next take-off is scheduled, check in the newspaper or telephone 1-800 432-2153.

Whether or not a launch is imminent, it's well worth visiting **Spaceport USA** (the visitor facilities) at the Kennedy Space Center, just off NASA Causeway linking Route A1A with the US Highway 1. The **Rocket Garden** includes several of the earliest research vehicles and also the kind of launchers that put the first Americans into orbit. It's remarkable how small they look now. You can climb aboard the *Ambassador*, a full size Space Shuttle used as a trainer.

The **Astronauts' Memorial** honours those who have died in accidents during the course of the space programme, and in a significant blend of technology and sculpture, it turns with the sun so that the light is reflected to illuminate their

*F*orty years of spacecraft have come to rest in the Rocket Garden at the John F Kennedy Space Center.

names. Multi-media exhibits and shows explain the amazing technology of space travel, and there is a chunk of real moon rock on display.

There's no charge for the basic visit, but you do have to pay to go on the bus tours and to see the IMAX films. Join the queue for tickets as soon as you can, planning what you want to do before you get to the ticket window. The **Red Bus Tour** takes you to the highlights of the moon landing programme, including the gigantic 520ft (158m) **Vehicle Assembly Building** (VAB), or the world's biggest 'room'. You won't be able to get close if a shuttle is being prepared for launch, and the bus route **95** may vary for operational reasons, but if all is well, you will be able to inspect a huge multi-stage Saturn moon rocket, left over when the last missions were cancelled, as well as the lunar launch pad. At **Mission Control**, a roomful of desks and screens, the technology looks quite archaic by more modern standards – perhaps that's why it worked.

The **Blue Bus Tour**, probably more suitable for fanatical

fans of rocketry, deals with the history of the unmanned rocket programme.

The 40-minute **IMAX films** projected on a giant 5-storey screen are truly thrilling. *The Dream is Alive* (also shown at the Air & Space Museum in Washington DC) is the story of the Space Shuttle, with a lot of footage shot by the astronauts themselves, inside and outside the orbiting craft. *Blue Planet* is stunningly beautiful as well as being a riveting lesson in geography.

The first astronauts used to relax, swim and surf at **Cocoa Beach**, on the strip of island to the south of the Kennedy Space Center. You could take a leaf out of their book and do the same, though the resort is a lot bigger now. The dunes also make an excellent viewpoint for watching shuttles launch into space.

Sunning or surfing at Cocoa Beach, south of Cape Canaveral, they'll soon sit up and take notice if there's a space launch.

BUSCH GARDENS

(Take the I-4 highway west to Tampa and exit at I-75. From the I-75 take exit 54 and follow the signs)

Only a 75-minute drive from Walt Disney World, in a huge 300-acre (120ha) park north east of Tampa, brewing giants Anheuser-Busch have mounted up the attractions as if trying to outdo all their rivals put together. The theme is turn-of-the-century Africa, with over 3,400 animals to view, as well as authentic **Moroccan-style architecture**. It's wise to collect the map at the entrance, as the layout is confusing.

The main attraction is the 80-acre (32ha) open plain of the **Serengeti**, with big game animals and herds of grazing zebras and antelopes viewed from cable-cars, a monorail or an old-fashioned train. There's also an extensive petting zoo for smaller children, and the park emphasizes its continuing committment to breeding endangered species.

At **Myombe Reserve: the Great Ape Domain**, you can **97**

hear the call of the wild, where lowland gorillas and chimpanzees reside in their natural environment (it's a good idea to take the self-guided tour).

A British bi-plane down in the Sahara? No, this is Busch **98** Gardens, near Tampa.

Meanwhile, the **World of Birds** show is one of the best in Florida – not to be missed.

When you've had enough of animals, you can get wet whilst **white water rafting** on River Congo, screaming down the **Tanganyika Tidal Wave**, with a 55ft (17m) drop, or heading down **Stanley Falls**, a log flume ride. Then you can turn your world upside down on the Python, Scorpion, or Kumba – three death-defying **roller coasters**, or take small children to another area with tamer rides.

There are shows all over the place, including an **ice show**, as well as **Questor**, a thrilling simulator ride. After all the excitement, you can visit the on-site **brewery** and sample the beers at Hospitality House (but only if you are 21 or over).

A mile (1.5km) from Busch Gardens, **Adventure Island** is a waterpark that offers waterfalls, waterslides, waves, and the Aruba Tuba, opened in 1993, a 420ft (128m) tunnels slide. The park closes in winter and is open weekends only during autumn.

What to Do

Several coffee cups in Disney theme parks carry pictures of Mickey Mouse, head in hands in apparent despair, and bearing the caption: 'There's so much to *do* here!' How right he is – but don't worry. Accept that you'll have to pick and choose and revel in the range of possibilities. In the summer in particular, take time off for complete relaxation, perhaps by the hotel pool, and enjoy some of the sports opportunities and entertainment outside the theme parks.

Sports

In Florida's delightful climate, watersports are a natural. Even in winter, the sun will tempt you out on most days, and the swimming pools will be warm. Most guests never see the golf courses at Walt Disney World – of course some golfers never see the theme parks! Add plenty of tennis courts, fishing and a host of other sporting facili-

ties and you have a marvellous sports resort.

Boating, Canoeing and Waterskiing

Walt Disney World is a web of waterways connecting lakes large and small, and almost all of its resorts are on a lake or canal, with their own landing places, or fully fledged marinas. To quote Mr Toad's friend the water rat, the park is just perfect for 'messing about in boats', and hundreds of pleasure craft of a dozen different sorts can be hired.

For **sailing**, conditions are best at two big lakes (Seven Seas Lagoon and Bay Lake at the Magic Kingdom Resorts). Both single hulls and catamarans are available. The same locations also have tow boats, drivers and all the equipment necessary for **waterskiing**.

The canals around Fort Wilderness are good for **canoeing**, and you can take **pedalos** on the lakes. If you prefer a motor to do the work, take a nippy mini-speedboat, a gentler motorized raft, canopy- or rubber **99** boat. Life jackets are provided at all locations.

Outside Walt Disney World, several resort hotels have lakes and watersports opportunities, or try Ski Holidays (on Lake Bryan Drive) with waterskiing and jet skiing; Splash 'n' Ski (Turkey Lake Road) with sailing, boating and waterskiing; or Airboat Rentals (on Vine Street, Kissimmee) with airboats and canoes for rental.

Fishing

Stocking of Florida's lakes and canals as well as strict environmental policies mean that fish have flourished. Guests at Walt Disney World are usually surprised to find that fishing is allowed from the shores at Fort Wilderness, and in the canals of the Village Resort (but it is, of course, carefully controlled).

In addition, a few people are taken on Bay Lake in organized expeditions every day, starting at 8am as well as one or two later times. Reservations are required and the cost is quite high, but there will be a good chance of catching sizeable bass. Tackle, bait and refreshments are provided.

Outside Walt Disney World, Florida is the perfect place for freshwater lakes and rivers: try Lake Tohopekaliga (or Toho) in Kissimmee.

Golf

With the 1992 opening of two new golf courses, Walt Disney World became the biggest golf resort in Florida: they call it the 'Magic Linkdom'. The five 18-hole championship courses enjoy a high reputation with professionals as well as amateurs, and there is also a 9-hole course intended for families and novices. Fees are relatively high for Florida (they are reduced if you can start after 3pm), but facilities are generally 'top hole'. Except for the 9-hole walking course, you must hire a cart.

The **Magnolia** and **Palm** courses flank the Disney Inn, near the Magic Kingdom, with the 9-hole **Executive** course adjoining the Magnolia. The **Lake Buena Vista** course, a

You can take to the water in a dozen different ways along the Florida coastline.

little narrower and shorter, is in the Disney Village, with its own clubhouse.

The newer **Bonnet Creek Golf Club**, in wooded country just north of Dixie Landings Resort, boasts the **Eagle Pines** and **Osprey Ridge** courses. Although each course has its own character, they're all par-72 and play about 7,000yd (6,400m) from the championship tees. Just because some bunkers are shaped like Mickey's ears doesn't make them any easier to escape – Disney courses have long been used on the US pro tour.

You can rent or buy anything you need for a game of golf from the pro shops at each club, and there's even a video-assisted 'clinic' at the Magnolia driving range. Lessons with resident professionals can also be arranged.

Outside Walt Disney World, Orlando has plenty of other golf courses. Try the Hyatt Regency Grand Cypress or the Marriott World Center resort hotels as well as several country clubs, such as the Orange Lake Country Club in Kissimmee, and Timacuan Golf and Country Club, Lake Mary.

Swimming

Apart from the **waterparks**, River Country (see p.59) and Typhoon Lagoon (see p.58), every resort and hotel in Walt Disney World has at least one pool. Many are imaginatively themed around ruined pirate forts, beached ships, grottoes and mountains, with fun slides for the children. If you want to swim serious laps, the sheer numbers of children can be an obstacle except at the big open pools of the Swan, the Dolphin and the Contemporary Resort.

Then there are the **beaches**. Walt Disney World may be an hour's drive from the sea, but the lakeside resorts have fine, white sandy shores, trees to provide ample shade, sunbeds to lie on – and the lake water is pure and clean.

Lifeguards are on duty (if not, there will be a sign notifying you of their absence). Disney hotels' pools or beaches are open only to guests staying at Disney-owned accommodation, but many other resort hotels have excellent facilities and most budget hotels or motels have some sort of pool.

Outside Walt Disney World, the exciting waterpark **Wet 'n' Wild** (see p.86) makes for an excellent day out, and **Cocoa Beach**, next to Cape Canaveral, has a fine beach with yearly surfing championships. Further south, making up just a part of the 100 miles (160km) of beaches, you'll find Satellite Beach and Indialantic Beach, which will be less crowded.

Tennis

Over two dozen tennis courts are scattered around the Walt Disney World Resort – at the Grand Floridian and Contemporary Resorts, the Disney Inn and Fort Wilderness; between the Swan and Dolphin and at the Yacht and Beach Clubs, and at the Village Clubhouse. Probably because most of the guests are either focussed on the parks or resting from their efforts therein, you will generally have no problem in making a court reservation.

Tennis rackets and balls can be bought or hired, and if you really want to improve your strokes, sign up for lessons and the video-monitored clinic at the Contemporary Resort.

Outside Walt Disney World, the big resort hotels and country clubs all have courts. Try the Orange Lake Country Club in Kissimmee, or the Orlando Tennis Center.

Other Activities

Volleyball has caught on in Florida: you can play at the Walt Disney World beaches, as well as at Typhoon Lagoon (see p.58) and Fort Wilderness, which also has **basketball** courts (or you can watch the Orlando Magic basketball team in the Arena).

Jogging route maps can be bought at Walt Disney World hotels – the most scenic routes are round the lake at Caribbean Beach, at Disney Village and at Fort Wilderness. You can hire **bicycles** at the Caribbean Beach, at Dixie Landings, Port Orleans and Fort Wilderness Resorts, as well as **103**

at the Recreation Center in Disney Village.

Health clubs complete with exercise machines, classes and other facilities are provided at most resorts in and around Orlando. Guests at Disney will find them at the Contemporary Resort, Grand Floridian, Dolphin, Swan, Yacht and Beach Clubs and Disney Inn.

Trail riding on placid horses is offered at Fort Wilderness, or try Poinciana Riding Stables at Kissimmee. Alternatively, you can go **walking** and **bird-spotting** along Fort Wilderness' nature trails, and **ice-skating** is a whizz at Orlando Ice Skating Palace or the Ice Rink International.

Shopping

Because so many shops are inside the theme parks, side-by-side with the attractions (and sometimes attractions in themselves!), shopping is often just a matter of checking out what is on offer near to the attraction or ride where you are. The shopping opportunities don't end there, however, and many more places to spend are located outside the parks, where you don't need a ticket and the parking is free.

At **Disney Village Marketplace**, near the Village Resort and next to Pleasure Island, 18 tree-shaded shops are arranged along the waterfront. Various restaurants nearby mean you can combine a trip with lunch or dinner.

Mickey's Character Shop has the biggest collection of Disney merchandise: clothes, toys, games and countless souvenirs. Nearby, the shops of **Pleasure Island** are open from 10am and you're free to explore them until 7pm – and to cast an eye over the rest of the island in the light of day.

Some of the odder outlets in Walt Disney World are here, and they're liable to change names and goods at short notice, so any list may soon date. Among the long term survivors look for: **Suspended Animation**, original and repro Disney art, and **Jessica's**, accessories themed around the lissom Jessica Rabbit.

*F*lorida's Atlantic and Gulf coasts offer endless sandy beaches which are an easy drive from Orlando.

Most of the Walt Disney World shops are designed to sell gifts and souvenirs, or more expensive collectibles. If you are just in need of a typical shopping centre right up close to Walt Disney World, albeit a good one, go to **Crossroads of Lake Buena Vista**, situated at the end of the road where most of the Village Plaza 'official' hotels are located (or leave the I-4 Highway at SR536 heading north, and turn immediately right). Here you'll find an excellent supermarket with a delicatessen counter, a café and pharmacy, a post office, bookstore, bank, dry cleaners, shoe and **105** clothes shops, and plenty of quick-service restaurants.

For some serious clothing shopping, you'll need to take a trip outside of Walt Disney World to one of the monster **shopping malls** in Orlando – concrete and metal agglomerations of many famous-name stores which demand almost as much stamina from you as the theme parks.

Here are a few of the main ones: Florida Mall is on Sand Lake Road north of International Drive; Fashion Square Mall is close to downtown Orlando on East Colonial Drive; The Exchange at Old Town and Church Street Station on route US192 has many shops in amongst the restaurants and entertainment (see p.87).

In addition, each suburb has shopping malls of their own. Park Avenue in Winter Park, north of Orlando, has smart and fashionable shopping with the likes of Laura Ashley and Crabtree & Evelyn.

Discount and **'factory outlet' malls** could be worth a visit, if you have the time to 106 rummage through 'pile-'em-high-sell-'em-cheap' stocks to find what you want. Try Belz Factory Outlet Mall and Quality Outlet Center, both off International Drive.

Entertainment

Of course, Walt Disney World is another word for entertainment (see p.27 for particular parades), but outside the resort most tastes will be catered for somewhere in the vast Orlando-Kissimmee area. Check the *Orlando Sentinel*, especially at weekends, for full listings of **concerts** – rock, pop or symphony, ballet, opera and theatre by local or touring groups.

If you have the energy to **dance** after a hard day at the theme parks, clubs and discos operate until 2am. JJ Whispers (Lee Road, Orlando) combines shows, a nightclub and a disco in one multi-storey complex. Church Street Station does the same both sides of an old arcaded downtown street. Alternatively, Wolfman Jack's, Old Town, Kissimmee offers live rock 'n' roll, and Sullivan's

Trailways Lounge is a country and western dance arena.

Dinner Shows

Food and entertainment packages at an inclusive price are all the rage in the Orlando vacation belt, and some of Disney's resorts offer their own versions. You don't have to be staying there to go either – you simply need a reservation.

That may not be easy for the popular **Hoop-Dee-Doo Musical Revue** at Fort Wilderness Campground, which offers energetic song, dance and comedy in Wild West style, as well as food which is big on 'country cookin''.

The **Polynesian Revue** at the Polynesian Resort is the kind of show you might expect to see in Hawaii, with South Seas cuisine adapted to American palates. The same entertainers, along with some of the Disney characters, also present **Mickey's Tropical Revue** for children in the late afternoon.

On top of the Contemporary Resort, **Broadway at the Top** accompanies dinner with music for dancing and some favourite show numbers.

You can eat and be entertained at the EPCOT Center too, in the Marrakesh (Morocco pavilion, see p.48), and also the Biergarten (German pavilion, see p.47).

Outside Walt Disney World, dinner shows will probably be more raucous, fuelled by unlimited beer or wine. Prices are competitive, there's plenty to eat, and the service is efficient. They've had plenty of practice, doing the same thing each night, but the entertainers manage to keep up a high level of enthusiasm.

Among a dozen options are: **Medieval Times** (Highway 192, Kissimmee), a jousting tournament with expert horsemanship; **King Henry's Feast** (International Drive, Orlando), with the much-married monarch in rollicking form; **Brazil Carnival** (Republic Drive, Orlando), featuring dancers and costumes from Rio; and **Arabian Nights** (Kissimmee, W Irlo Bronson Memorial Highway) starring horses, acrobatic riders and chariot races. **107**

Pleasure Island

Conscious that they were losing guests in the evenings to outside attractions, the Disney organization decided to create nightlife of its own. **Pleasure Island** is the result: a complex of bars and dance halls, comedy acts and live bands. The setting is designed like a run-down, ramshackle port which has been given an expensive facelift. Restaurants and nightclubs inhabit the 'old' warehouses and some of the action takes place in the streets.

You can visit the area free of charge during the day, and the restaurants at any time. To gain entry to any of the nightclubs, you need a ticket, which can be bought at the main entrance point (unless you hold a 5-day Super Pass including admission to Pleasure Island).

The clubs open around 7pm (although you won't see too much action from the guests at that early hour), and keep going non-stop until 2am. It's hard to predict which will be the liveliest, or when. People tend to hop from one to the other, checking them out, then settling somewhere by 10 or 11pm. Upstairs, the **Mannequins Dance Palace**, with its rotating floor and elaborate lighting system, is the smartest disco. **X-ZFR** (say 'zephyr') **Rock and Roll Beach Club** features live rock bands and a disco when the musicians are taking a break. Live country music rules at **Neon Armadillo**, and you'll be wrapped up in 'progressive' MTV underground at **Cage**.

The **Adventurers' Club** is an oddity. Is it a museum? A bar? A piece of theatre, or an eccentrics' hangout? It seems sometimes that nothing is happening, and you can sit over a drink and study the jokey relics of outlandish 'expeditions'. But then some strange character may appear and start to regale you with tall stories. Watch out for special effects: some things may not be quite what they seem.

You will probably have to queue to get into the **Comedy Warehouse**. Hopeful potential comedians as well as some established stand-up comics appear in shows on the hour from 7pm to 1am.

You need to be aged 18 or over to get into the nightclubs (it's 21 in the case of Mannequins Dance Palace and Cage), and 21 or over to be served alcohol. Carry your passport (or US driver's licence) as proof.

In Downtown Orlando, the **Church Street Station** enter-

*H*undreds of miles of quiet inland waterways are just perfect for canoeing.

tainment complex also offers plenty of nightlife (see p.87).

Films

If you're looking for some more sedentary entertainment, all the latest movie releases (not only Disney's) are at the 10-screen **AMC** complex next to Pleasure Island.

Ticket prices are lower for early evening shows. Disney classics as well as new features are also screened occasionally at resort hotels and Fort Wilderness.

Eating Out

New arrivals are hardly able to believe the sheer scale of it all. So much to eat, so many places to choose from. Florida is a major producer of beef, fish and shellfish, salad crops and vegetables, a world leader in growing citrus fruit, and the best restaurants take advantage of the fresh local produce.

Fierce competition means that you'll usually get good value for money, especially in the type of food America does well: steaks, barbecues, fried chicken, combined with a buffet or salad bar. Menus from Italy, China, Japan and a dozen other national styles add variety. See the list of recommended restaurants on pp.73-80.

In the theme parks, the only reason to go hungry would be if you were too busy having fun to stop for food. Opportunities for eating are countless, from snacks to elegant dinners. Parks in the past were accused of dishing up only fast food laced with fat and sugar, but now the choice is more varied.

The old faithfuls are still available, but the overall style is healthier, with plenty of salads and fresh fruit, and frozen yoghurt as well as ice-cream. Buffets and full-service restaurants in the theme parks and hotels also cater for mainstream tastes and are rarely adventurous, but especially in Disney territory, the decor is frequently half the fun.

During the day, most visitors don't want to use up time sitting down to a long lunch. They may get a snack from a vendor's cart and then join the queue for one of the rides, or line up for a salad or fast-food at a counter or cafeteria.

In fact, bowing to the inevitable, even the main full-service restaurants offer mainly simple dishes and sandwiches at lunchtime.

THE MAGIC KINGDOM

There are only two restaurants in the Magic Kingdom which accept advance reservations at the door: King Stefan's Banquet Hall in Cinderella Castle, and Tony's Town Square.

If you're in more of a hurry, The Crystal Palace is a convenient cafeteria near the central Plaza, and Tomorrowland Terrace is a major quick-service operation. You'll find fast food stalls dotted all over the park.

Note: no alcoholic drinks are served in the Magic Kingdom.

THE EPCOT CENTER

You wouldn't go to the Magic Kingdom just to eat, but you might to the EPCOT Center (see pp.73-80 for a list of restaurants). Future World has the usual fast food and snack stalls as well as two full-service restaurants, but the difference at EPCOT is that each of the countries in World Showcase runs at least one restaurant.

You will need reservations for almost all of the full-service restaurants, which can be made at the Earth Station information centre, on the touch-sensitive screens. This must be done on the day, and as soon as you can for the popular places. Lunch reservations are easier, and can be made at the restau-

rants themselves as well as at Earth Station.

Note: guests in Disney-owned accommodation can telephone in advance for reservations.

Future World

The two full-service restaurants here are the Land pavilion's Land Grille and the Coral Reef Restaurant in the Living Seas pavilion.

Elsewhere in Future World, you'll find standard fare in both West and East Communi-Core buildings and the Odyssey complex next to World of Motion, and snacks at Pure & Simple in Wonders of Life.

World Showcase

Here we'll follow the same clockwise order as on pp.46-49. In **Mexico** the **San Angel Inn**, overlooking the River of Time boat ride, is an offshoot of a famous Mexico City restaurant. It offers more than the usual Mexican fare found in the US, though the spices are mild by the standards of the **111**

*P*utting on the glitz – shop all night if you like at Cocoa Beach (above). Or you may think you've strayed into a 1950s time warp at Universal Studios (right).

original cuisine. The informal **Cantina de San Angel** by the lagoon does, however, have the more familiar tacos, tortillas and beans.

In the **Norway** pavilion, the **Restaurant Akershus** puts on a magnificent colourful buffet, from salted and spiced herring to hot and cold entrées, Nor-

wegian cheeses and delicious desserts.

China's **Nine Dragons** restaurant offers various regional styles which range from spicy Szechuan to the more familiar (to British diners at least!) Cantonese cuisine.

In the **Germany** pavilion, the courtyard **Biergarten** has wursts, dumplings, sauerkraut roasts and big steins of beer, plus entertainment by yodellers, musicians and dancers.

L'Originale Alfredo di Roma Ristorante in **Italy** runs the standard gamut from pastas to *gelati.*

Liberty Inn flies the flag for basic **American** burgers, big sandwiches and old-fashioned apple pie.

In the **Japan Teppanyaki Dining Rooms**, you sit round a flat grill where a chef stir-fries the food of their choice. The **Tempura Kiku** serves light, deep-fried seafood and vegetables and the **Yakitori House** specializes in grills. Meanwhile, the **Matsu No Ma** lounge caters for the growing numbers of *sushi* fans.

Morocco's **Marrakesh** restaurant features couscous and kebabs, roast lamb and sweet honeyed desserts.

France's choice is between the elegant **Chefs de France**, comfortable **Bistro de Paris**, and the open-air **Au Petit Café** (where you don't need to make a reservation, but may have to wait for a table).

The **United Kingdom** is represented by the traditional-style **Rose & Crown Dining Room** where you can fill up with fish and chips, steak and kidney pie, traditional English trifle and English cheeses.

Very conveniently for those without reservations, **Le Cellier**, in the **Canada** pavilion, is a cafeteria (sometimes there is a long queue). Familiar roasts, salmon and salads are augmented by French-Canadian dishes, Canadian cheeses and maple syrup with desserts.

113

DISNEY-MGM STUDIOS

Here, the food is mostly all-American – even the Italian and the chilli – served up amid themed designs and entertainment, and 30s to 50s fashion. You can make reservations for the four full-service restaurants (see p.58) at their doors: Mama Melrose's, the Sci-Fi Drive-In Diner, the Hollywood Brown Derby Grill and the 50s Prime Time Café.

For those who don't want to eat when they might be queueing for important attractions, fast-food stalls and carts are scattered round the park.

HOTELS

All the Disney hotels provide the stand-bys which guests expect, but menus also emphasize the themes which make them all a bit different (see pp.66-72 for our listing).

One or two out-of-the-ordinary establishments are the Palio in the Walt Disney World Swan; Harry's Grill in the Walt Disney World Dolphin; and The Beach Club's Cape May Café, with its clambake every night.

ELSEWHERE IN WALT DISNEY WORLD

Although the clubs on **Pleasure Island** don't open until 7pm, restaurants operate from 11am, and snack spots earlier.

At **Disney Village Marketplace**, the riverboat *Empress Lilly* (named in honour of Lillian, Walt Disney's wife), has a choice of three restaurants. Fisherman's Deck has crab, snapper, lobster and speciality seafood (scallops, shrimp) as well as pasta and fresh vegetables). Carnivores go for Steerman's Quarters for prime rib and steaks, and the (pricey) Empress Room has one of the most elegant settings imaginable, in Louis XV style, and a menu recalling grand hotel-restaurants of the past.

Disney Village Marketplace itself offers more choices. The independent Plaza hotels have their own restaurants, and the **Crossroads at Lake Buena Vista** has another selection of non-Disney food outlets.

BLUEPRINT
for a
Perfect Trip

An A–Z Summary of Practical Information and Facts

Certain items of information in this section will already be familiar to US residents, but have been included to be of help to visitors from overseas.

A

ACCOMMODATION (See also CAMPING on p.118, YOUTH HOSTELS on p.141, and the list of RECOMMENDED HOTELS starting on p.66)

In high season reservations may be hard to come by, especially at Walt Disney World. Book in advance: even a year may not be too much for Christmas and Easter. State taxes are extra (see p.66).

American hotels/motels usually charge by room, rather than number of occupants. Most rooms have two double beds, a private bathroom and colour television. 'Efficiencies' are rooms with kitchenette or separate kitchen and dining area, with dishes, pans and cutlery.

Peak periods in Orlando are: mid-December to early January; February to April (including Easter); and early June to mid-August. At other times, prices are slightly lower in some Disney accommodations, and may be much lower in non-Disney properties.

Some resort hotels offer special rates to guests who take meals on the premises: American Plan includes three meals a day, while Modified American Plan covers breakfast and either lunch or dinner.

Larger hotels employ a concierge who can arrange tours, call a taxi or hire a car for you. Visitors on a budget can economize by making their own arrangements.

AIRPORTS

Orlando (McCoy) International Airport (code ORL or MCO) is 9 miles (15km) south of downtown Orlando and about 25 miles (40km) from Walt Disney World. Spacious, glittering and constantly expanding, it has three terminals, with satellite gates reached by 'peoplemover' shuttle trains. There are no baggage trolleys, so although carrying distances are short, wheels are desirable. Disney characters make appearances during the day to greet and wave goodbye to travellers.

Ground Transport (see also p.140). Taxis and less expensive shuttle minibuses ply between the airport and Walt Disney World locations, International Drive, downtown Orlando, Kissimmee and Cocoa Beach. Some hotels operate free shuttle services to and from the airport (check with them) and if you are on a package tour, airport transfers may be included. There's a public bus to downtown Orlando.

Check-in Time. Arrive 45 minutes before domestic flights, and at least 1 hour before international flights (airlines suggest 2 hours). For flight information, telephone your airline.

Other Florida airports. Miami, Tampa, Fort Lauderdale, West Palm Beach and Key West also have international airports.

Domestic Flights. Air travel is by far the quickest and most convenient way of getting around the US. Travellers from abroad can buy a Visit USA ticket, which gives substantial discounts and sets no fixed programme. To benefit, you must buy these before you arrive in the US (or within 15 days of arrival).

Fares change constantly, so it would be wise to consult travel agents for the latest information about special deals.

B

BICYCLE RENTAL

Bikes are available for hire at several Disney accommodations including Fort Wilderness and the Caribbean Beach, Dixie Landings and Port Orleans Resorts. Locks are included.

CAMPING

Camping American-style generally involves recreational vehicles ('RVs') such as campers, motor homes or caravans (trailers). If you are camping the American way, the *Rand McNally Campground and Trailer Park Guide* and *Woodalls* both list and grade campgrounds and their facilities. (Incidentally, 'campsite' in the US means the specific spot where you put your 'RV' or tent.) Camping by the road, or on private land without permission, is both illegal and unsafe.

Disney's Fort Wilderness Resort has sites where you can put up a tent or park your trailer or 'RV'. If you don't have either, 'trailer homes' (fairly luxurious, air-conditioned chalets) are available. You will need a reservation.

CAR RENTAL

Competition keeps rates relatively low. Reserving a car before you arrive is often cheaper. Rental companies are found at all Florida's bigger airports, and it's possible to rent a car at one airport and return it to another. Major operators run buses from airports to their offices.

The well-known rental agencies have higher rental rates, but may include insurance costs in the price; smaller agencies may have little or no insurance included in the rates. You are advised to ensure you have CDW (collision damage waiver), or you will be charged for some/all repairs, regardless of whose fault the collision was. Many inclusive holidays and fly-drive packages promise a 'free car', but you usually have to pay Florida taxes and CDW when you collect it.

To rent a car you must be over 21 (sometimes 25) with a valid driving licence. Some agencies make exceptions for 18-year-old drivers paying by credit card. For tourists from non-English-speaking countries, a translation of the driving licence is recommended, together with the national licence itself or an International Driving Permit.

It is generally more convenient to pay with a major credit card than with cash. If you have no card, a deposit will be required. **118** Sometimes cash is refused at night and weekends.

CHILDREN

Florida in general and Orlando's theme parks in particular should be a paradise for children. The rides themselves will appeal to them, but also the hotel pools, games and the crowds of their peers.

In the parks, walking distances are quite long but pushchairs (strollers) are available for rent. The sun, heat and humidity can take their toll, especially due to long waits for popular attractions. Small and nervous children could be disturbed by some rides: take advice from the staff. Even the famous Disney characters can seem frightening to the very young. It might be worth warning children that the characters don't speak! The following is a list of rides in the theme parks that small children may find stressful: Walt Disney World's Space Mountain, Big Thunder Mountain Railroad, and the EPCOT Center's Body Wars; Universal Studios' Back to The Future; Disney-MGM Studios' Star Tours; and Sea World's Bermuda Triangle.

Restaurants are used to catering to all ages, and many larger hotels provide a **babysitting** service, playgroups and special entertainment.

CLIMATE

Winter is usually delightful in central Florida, but there are rainy days and cold spells – temperatures *can* dip to freezing. On the other hand, winter temperatures can reach the 80s F (30°C), so be sure to pack clothing for every eventuality.

Summer ranges from hot to very hot, with high humidity. From June to October, it rains most days, though it is rarely troublesome. Hurricanes are rare. On average, Florida is hit one year in seven and only between July and November, so the chances of your experiencing one are minimal. For a weather report, dial (407) 824-4104.

	J	F	M	A	M	J	J	A	S	O	N	D
°C	21	22	24	26	30	31	31	31	30	29	25	23
°F	70	72	76	79	86	87	87	87	86	84	77	73

The above chart shows average maximum daytime temperatures for Orlando (the US still works on the Fahrenheit scale). **119**

CLOTHING

When it starts to get hot or sticky, Floridians turn on the air-conditioners. These can blow with arctic chill, so don't forget to take a wrap with you when shopping, dining out or riding in air-conditioned vehicles – including buses.

Casual wear is appropriate round the clock – something light, bright, loose and made of cotton rather than artificial fibres. If you're likely to go swimming often, bring spare swimwear for a rapid change. Other useful items to pack include an umbrella and comfortable walking or sports shoes.

In theme parks and their transportation, footwear and a shirt or equivalent top cover are required.

COMPLAINTS

If something goes wrong, you'll probably be able to sort it out on the spot with the well-trained, helpful personnel who are typical of the service industries in Florida, and especially in the well-run theme parks. If they can't deal with your problem, ask for someone more senior. Disney accommodations all have a special service telephone number to call in case of difficulties. In the theme parks, the Guest Services desks will assist you.

CRIME

The big theme parks have their own security personnel, so discreet that you are hardly ever aware of them, but they'll be on hand if you need them. Walt Disney World is probably one of the safest environments on earth, but that doesn't mean you shouldn't look after your property. Lockers are available at all theme parks. Most hotels have a safe for valuables. Never leave money, credit cards, cheque books, cameras, etc in a hotel room – always use the safe.

Outside the theme parks, beware of pickpockets. Carjackings and highway crimes are also quite frequent: be aware. Buying and selling illegal drugs is a serious offence and Florida has a large force of undercover police officers who are battling to keep drugs out. If you are robbed, tell the police, and obtain a copy of the report for your insurance company.

Report stolen credit cards and travellers' cheques immediately. (You should have kept a separate copy of the numbers. Ideally, carry a copy of your airline ticket and passport as well.)

CUSTOMS and ENTRY REGULATIONS

British (UK citizens) and some other foreign visitors no longer require a visa to enter the US, and instead can obtain a visa waiver form from their travel agent or airline. Canadians need only evidence of their nationality. Citizens of the Republic of Ireland, Australia, New Zealand and South Africa need a visa (but these rules can change, so check with your US Embassy or Consulate, or travel agent). The application process can be slow, depending on individual circumstances. When you apply, take documents along which show that you intend to return home.

Duty-Free Allowance. You will be asked to fill out a customs declaration form before you arrive in the US. The following chart shows what main duty-free items you may take into the US (if you are over 21) and, when returning home, back into your own country.

Currency restrictions. A non-resident may take in, free of duty and taxes, articles of up to $100 in value for use as gifts. Don't arrive with any plants, seeds, fruits or other fresh food, as they're banned. The same goes for liqueur chocolates. Arriving and departing passengers should report any money or cheques totalling over $10,000.

INTO	Cigarettes	Cigars	Tobacco	Spirits	Wine
USA	200 or	50 or	1350 g	1 litre or	1 litre
Australia	200 or	250 g or	250 g	1 litre or	1 litre
Canada	200 and	50 and	900 g	1.1 litre or	1.1 litre
Eire	200 or	50 or	250 g	1 litre and	2 litres
N Zealand	200 or	50 or	250 g	1.1 litre and	4.5 litres
S Africa	400 and	50 and	250 g	1 litre and	2 litres
UK	200 or	50 or	250 g	1 litre and	2 litres

DISABLED TRAVELLERS

Accessibility and facilities are excellent at the theme parks and other attractions in Orlando. Special parking is available near the entrances to each park, to the hotels and other facilities.

Disney publishes a special *Disabled Guests Guidebook*. Ask at City Hall in the Magic Kingdom and at Information/Guest Services desks in other areas.

Wheelchairs are available for rent in limited numbers in several locations: Magic Kingdom, at the Stroller Shop just inside the main entrance; the EPCOT Center, at the base of Spaceship Earth and at International Gateway; Disney-MGM Studios, just inside the main entrance at Oscar's Super Service. At Sea World and Universal Studios Florida, they may be rented at the entrance. For some attractions and rides, guests may remain in wheelchairs: for others they may have to be able to leave the wheelchair. Regulations are clearly indicated in leaflets and at the appropriate entrance. Some motorized wheelchairs are available for rent at the EPCOT Center, and some buses and launches can accommodate conventional, but not motorized wheelchairs. Wheelchair access is available at toilets in all the theme parks.

For hearing-impaired guests there is a TDD (Telecommunications Device for the Deaf) at City Hall (Magic Kingdom), at the Earth Center (the EPCOT Center) and at Guest Services, main entrance (Disney-MGM Studios).

Sight-impaired guests can borrow complimentary cassettes and tape recorders at the same locations. A deposit is required.

DRIVING

On the road. Drive on the right. In Florida, you may turn right after a stop at a red light, provided that there is no cross-traffic, you have given way to pedestrians, and there is no sign to the contrary. Headlights should be used when it is raining enough for window wipers. Front seatbelts must be worn and you must carry a driving licence.

Lane discipline differs from European norms. American drivers tend to stick to one lane, making no distinction between 'fast' or 'slow' lanes (except to some extent on the Interstate network). You may therefore be overtaken on either side, so don't change lanes without careful checking. In populated areas, the middle lane is generally for making left turns only.

Don't drink and drive – driving while intoxicated ('DWI') may get you locked up.

Expressways/motorways. On the high-speed divided highways (expressways), driving follows certain rules. Rather than accelerating up the slip road to join the traffic at its own speed, you hesitate at the top and wait for an opening. A speed limit of 55mph (90kmph) operates on highways, except on expressways in rural areas, where the limit is 65mph (105kmph). Other limits such as 45mph (70kmph) apply where indicated. If you keep up with the flow of traffic, you'll have no problem, but go any faster and you'll be pulled over.

If you break down on an expressway, pull over on to the right-hand shoulder, tie a handkerchief to the doorhandle or radio aerial, raise the bonnet and wait in the car for assistance. At night, use the hazard warning lights.

Tolls. Some of the various types of road in Florida (including the turnpike), as well as many causeways and bridges, collect tolls. Keep a supply of coins when travelling; most toll areas provide a basket into which you drop the correct coinage, so there's no waiting.

Petrol/gas and services. Florida's service stations have both self-service and full-service pumps, fuel at the latter being much more expensive. In some areas it is necessary to pre-pay, especially at night. Some pumps are operated by inserting a credit card (major international cards are accepted). Note that some stations close in the evening and on Sunday. In Walt Disney World, petrol (gas) stations can be found near the main entrance to the Magic Kingdom and at the Crossroads shopping centre.

Most rental cars in Florida are equipped with air-conditioners; if your car is running low on petrol (gas) or overheating, turn off the 'air-con' – it's a strain on the engine.

Distance

Fluid measures

Parking. All the theme parks provide extensive facilities for car parking. There is usually a charge, although at Disney parks it is free if you are staying at Disney-owned accommodation and display the card which you are given when you register. If you do have to pay a parking fee, keep the ticket, since it is valid for all parks used that day. Remember and always make a careful note of the exact spot where you leave your car.

In general, you should park facing in the direction of traffic flow, and nose-in when angle parking is indicated (because Florida cars have no front number plates). Never park next to a fire hydrant, or a kerb painted yellow or red.

Directions. Try to get help planning your route if you don't know the area you are crossing or heading for.

The American Automobile Association offers assistance to members of affiliated organizations abroad. It also provides travel information for the US and can arrange automobile insurance by the month for owner-drivers. Contact the AAA at 1000 AAA Drive, Heathrow, Florida FL 32746-5063; tel. (407) 444-7000.

Road signs. Although the US has started to use the standard international road signs, progress is gradual, and this can inevitably lead to some confusion. Detailed below are several common Anglo/American discrepancies:

American	British
Detour	Diversion
Divided highway	Dual carriageway
No passing	No overtaking
Railroad crossing	Level crossing
Traffic circle	Roundabout
Yield	Give way

E

ELECTRIC CURRENT
The US has 110-115 volt 60-cycle AC. Plugs are small, flat and two-pronged or (more rarely) three-pronged; foreigners will need an adaptor for shavers and some other electrical appliances.

EMBASSIES and CONSULATES
Few English-speaking countries maintain a consulate in Florida. The nearest ones to contact are listed below:

Australia: 636 5th Avenue, New York; tel. (212) 245-4000.
Canada: 1251 Avenue of the Americas, New York;
tel. (212) 596-1700.
New Zealand: Embassy, 37 Observatory Circle, NW, Washington DC; tel. (202) 328-4800.
Republic of Ireland: 345 Park Avenue, 17th Floor, New York;
tel. (212) 319-2555.
South Africa: 333 East 38th Street, New York; tel. (212) 213-4880.
United Kingdom: 245 Peachtree Street NE, Atlanta, Georgia;
tel. (404) 524-5856.

EMERGENCIES

(See also MEDICAL CARE on p.130 and POLICE on p.135)

Dial **911**, and the operator will ask if you want police, ambulance or the fire department. All towns and cities have a 24-hour number to call for emergency, if you need a doctor or a dentist.

First Aid posts in Walt Disney World are situated next to the Crystal Palace Restaurant, Main Street, USA (Magic Kingdom); Odyssey Complex, Future World (EPCOT); and the main entrance Guest Services (Disney-MGM Studios). In other areas, you should ask where they are sited.

ETIQUETTE

Foreign visitors will have to get used to American informality: don't be startled if the hotel desk clerk calls you by your first name. Many Americans are very polite, saying 'Sir' or 'Ma'am' to strangers and service staff. 'Thank you is answered by 'you're welcome' or 'you're quite welcome', 'quite' meaning 'very'.

GETTING TO ORLANDO

Since fares and conditions change frequently, it is advisable to consult travel agents for the latest information.

FROM WITHIN NORTH AMERICA

By air. There are non-stop or direct flights every day to Orlando and other major Florida cities from most large US cities.

By bus. Florida destinations are linked to all major centres by Greyhound, which has now absorbed its previous competitor, Trailways. (New York to Orlando by express coach takes around 25 hours.) Smaller bus lines provide a comprehensive local shuttle service between hotels and attractions, and also offer sightseeing tours. Be wary of long-distance, one-day tours: they don't always give suffi-

cient time to visit. Visitors can buy unlimited Rover passes (which are only obtainable outside the US), valid for a given length of time, to go anywhere in the country by bus at a flat rate.

By rail. Amtrak offers a variety of bargain fares including Excursion and Family fares, and tour packages with hotel and guide included. It runs a car-carrying train daily between Lorton, near Washington DC, and Sanford, near Orlando.

By car. Travellers coming down the east coast can take the I-95 route via Washington and Savannah. The shortest route from the west coast is the I-10, passing Tucson, El Paso, Houston and Mobile.

FROM THE UK

By air. There are many non-stop and other direct flights from Heathrow and Gatwick to Orlando and Miami. Fares available include first-class, economy, excursion, APEX (Advance Purchase Excursion), super-APEX, and special 'ticket sales' and promotions available through travel agents. In general, the longer ahead you book, the lower the fare, with the exception of standby fares, which only apply at certain times of year. Some US airlines offer travellers from abroad a discount on the cost of each internal flight, or flat-rate unlimited-travel tickets for specific periods.

Charter flights and package tours. Most charter flights must be booked and paid for well in advance. Many package tours are available: two-centre holidays divide their time between Orlando and one of the beaches (east or west coast). Other packages on offer combine Orlando with a short cruise, or a spell on a Caribbean island.

Baggage. Allowances for scheduled transatlantic flights are complex, but you are allowed to check in, free, two suitcases of normal size. In addition, one piece of hand baggage which fits easily under the aircraft seat may be carried on board. Confirm size and weight restrictions with your travel agent or air carrier when booking your ticket. It is advisable to insure all luggage for the duration of your trip, preferably as part of a combined travel insurance policy.

FROM ELSEWHERE IN EUROPE

Frankfurt, Amsterdam and Paris have non-stop services to Orlando. Many other European cities are linked to Florida by one-stop and other direct flights.

GUIDES and TOURS

Some of the larger attractions provide the services of a guide. In the Magic Kingdom, ask at City Hall (tours begin at 10.30am); in the EPCOT Center inquire at Earth Station. Foreign-language guides are on call to take visitors on a quick tour, including a selection of rides.

LANGUAGE

Most English-speaking foreigners are now familiar with American words and phrases. However, here are a few of the most common Anglo-American linguistic misunderstandings:

US	British
admission	entry fee
bathroom	toilet (private)
bill	banknote (money)
billfold	wallet
check	bill (restaurant)
collect call	reverse charge call
elevator	lift
faucet	tap
first floor	ground floor
gas(oline)	petrol
general delivery	poste restante
liquor	spirits
liquor store	off-licence
pants	trousers

pavement	road surface
purse/pocketbook	handbag
restroom	toilet (public)
second floor	first floor
sidewalk	pavement
stand in line	queue up
stroller	pushchair
subway	underground
trailer	caravan
underpass	subway
undershirt	vest
vest	waistcoat

LAUNDRY and DRY CLEANING

Coin-operated washing machines and driers are available at all Disney accommodations and many other hotels. You can send laundry through most hotels from Monday to Saturday. It will be returned the same day if dropped off before 9am.

LOST PROPERTY

Each theme park has a Lost Property desk near the entrance. At hotels, ask at the Guest Services desk or telephone Housekeeping.

Air, rail and bus terminals and many stores have special Lost and Found areas. Restaurants put aside lost articles in the hope that someone will claim them. If your lost property is valuable, contact the police. If you lose your passport, get in touch with your consulate immediately (see p.125).

M

MAPS

The free Guidebook leaflets available at Guest Services/Information desks (City Hall in the Magic Kingdom, Earth Station at EPCOT, and the main entrances of Disney-MGM Studios, Universal Studios and Sea World) include excellent maps.

Florida Welcome Stations on main highways and ports of entry hand out free maps, and the chamber of commerce or the tourist authority will give you local maps with attractions marked on them. Service stations dispense maps from vending machines, and car rental agencies give out useful road maps.

MEDICAL CARE (See also EMERGENCIES on p.126)

Foreigners should note that the US does not provide free medical services, and that medical treatment is **expensive**. Arrangements should therefore be made in advance for temporary health insurance (through a travel agent or insurance company); alternatively, ask at your local Social Security office for precise information on coverage during your trip.

'Health-First' clinics offer less prohibitively expensive access to treatment than private practitioners. Emergency rooms of hospitals will treat anyone in need of speedy attention, including hospitalization in a community ward. Disney accommodations offer House Med, an in-room health-care service, but it has to be paid for.

Beware of the powerful **sun**. Start with a sunscreen with SPF20 or more, or a complete-block cream at first. Build up your tan gradually in small doses. (Sunscreen products can be bought at many Disney shops.) Drink plenty of water. You can quickly become dehydrated: the warning signs are headaches, lassitude – and grumpy children.

Visitors from the UK will find that some **medicines** sold over the counter at home can only be bought on prescription in the US. There's no shortage of drugstores, or pharmacies, and a few of them open late at night.

130   No **vaccinations** are required or recommended for Orlando.

MONEY MATTERS

Currency. The dollar is divided into 100 cents.

Banknotes: $1, $2 (rare), $5, $10, $20, $50 and $100. Larger denominations are not in general circulation. All notes are the same shape and colour, so it is wise to keep large and small notes in separate compartments of a wallet (ie don't stack $100 notes with $1 notes).

Coins: 1¢ (called a 'penny'), 5¢ ('nickel'), 10¢ ('dime'), 25¢ ('quarter'), 50¢ ('half dollar') and $1. Only the first four are commonly used. You may inadvertently be given Canadian coins in change. They're worth about 15% less than US ones, and they don't work in automatic machines, such as telephones.

'Disney dollars' in $1, $5 and $10 denominations are available at Walt Disney World ticket booths or Information/Guest Services desks. You can use them to pay for food and merchandise anywhere within the Walt Disney World Resort. They can be changed back to US dollars at any time. There's no actual *need* to buy them, unless you want one as a souvenir.

Banks and currency exchange. Banking hours are usually from 9am to 2 or 3pm Monday to Friday, but very few banks change foreign currency. Walt Disney World's banks are a notable exception: their hours are longer and they give a good rate of exchange. You'll find them at Town Square in the Magic Kingdom and the entrance to the EPCOT Center. In all three parks, the Guest Services desks can change many foreign currencies. Other bank branches are opposite Disney Village Marketplace and at the Crossroads of Lake Buena Vista shopping centre. Large hotels are also able to change foreign money. Elsewhere it is simpler as well as safer to travel with travellers' cheques (see p.132) denominated in dollars, major credit cards or cash in dollars.

When changing money or travellers' cheques, ask for $20 notes, which are accepted everywhere, as some establishments will refuse to accept larger notes unless they nearly equal the amount to be paid.

Credit cards. When buying merchandise and tickets, or paying hotel and phone bills, you will invariably be asked: 'Cash or charge?', meaning you have the choice of paying in cash or by credit card. Businesses are wary of little-known cards, but they'll gladly accept the top American and international cards. You'll often need some additional form of identification when charging your purchase. Some international cards will operate cash dispensers if you know the PIN number, and certain banks will advance cash against the card.

Many service stations will not take money at night, only cards. Outside normal office hours, it's sometimes impossible to rent cars and pay bills with cash.

Travellers' cheques are safer than cash. They can be exchanged quickly, as long as they are in US dollars. Banks will usually want to see your passport or another form of identity document, but many hotels, shops and restaurants will accept them directly in lieu of cash, especially those issued by American banks. Change small amounts at a time: keep the balance of your cheques in your hotel safe and make a note of serial numbers, and where and when you used each cheque.

Prices. Most displayed prices do not include the state sales tax of around 6% – it's added when you pay. The same applies to hotel bills, to which 10 or 11% is added.

The US has a larger spread of prices for the same kind of item than you might find elsewhere, as well as a greater choice. For moderately priced goods, visit the big department and discount stores. Small independent grocery stores, drugstores and 24-hour 'convenience stores' have price mark-ups of between 10 and 70% over the supermarkets, but independent service stations are cheaper than those of the large oil companies.

PLANNING YOUR BUDGET

To give you an idea of what to expect, here's a list of average prices. They can only be broad guidelines, since inflation continues to push prices upwards.

Airport transfer: Orlando International Airport to Walt Disney World: taxi $38, shuttle $13. Airport to International Drive: taxi $22, shuttle $11.

Babysitters: $5 per hour for one or two children, $1 for each additional child, plus transport expenses. Hotels including Disney properties charge $9 per hour.

Bicycle rental: $3 per hour, $8 per day, $35 per week.

Camping: Fort Wilderness: $35-52 per day, per site (space) with 'RV' hook-upt. Elsewhere: $15-20.

Car rental: Prices in Florida vary widely. A typical rate for a compact car, unlimited mileage and full insurance during high season might be $36 per day, $169 per week.

Entertainment: Cinema $4-8; nightclub/disco $5-20, including cover charge, $4-7 drinks; dinner and show $30-50.

Hotels (double room with bathroom): Walt Disney World: deluxe $240 and up, standard $150, moderate $69. Elsewhere: deluxe $150 and up, moderate $70-100, budget $40-80, motel $30-50.

Laundry: Shirt $1.90, blouse $3.75. Dry cleaning: jacket $4.50 and up, trousers $2.75 and up, dress $6 and up.

Meals and drinks: Continental breakfast $2-7, full breakfast $4-9, lunch in snack bar $5, in restaurant $7-14, dinner $15-30 (more with entertainment), coffee $1.50, beer $2-3, glass of wine $3-5, carafe of wine $6-10, bottle of wine $10-20, cocktail $4-6.

Petrol/gas: $1.30 per US gallon (approximately 4 litres).

Taxi (Orlando area): $2.25, plus $1.25 per mile.

Theme parks: One-day ticket (Magic Kingdom *or* Disney-MGM Studios *or* the EPCOT Center): $36, child aged 3-9 $29. Four-Day All Three Disney Parks Passport $141.55, child $113.05. Five-Day Plus Super Pass (all parks and other facilities) $189.15, child $151.05. Pleasure Island $15.85, Typhoon Lagoon $22.79, River Country $14.84, Discovery Island $10.07. Universal Studios one-day ticket $36, child $29. Sea World one-day ticket $35, child $30.

NEWSPAPERS and MAGAZINES

Local newspapers and the national daily *USA Today* are sold in drugstores and from vending machines. Special news-stands carry **133**

The New York Times and *The Wall Street Journal*, as well as a variety of other newspapers. The *Orlando Sentinel*, one of the better US newspapers, provides information about central Florida and gives TV programmes, opening hours of attractions, pages of grocery store bargains, and coupons for price reductions at various restaurants. Newspapers and magazines from Britain, Germany, France, Italy etc are usually available the day following publication in some big supermarkets, shops and hotels.

OPENING HOURS

The three Disney theme parks advertize their opening time as 9am, but that applies to the rides and other attractions. The **Magic Kingdom's Main Street, USA** is open at 8am and the gates at the **EPCOT Center** and **Disney-MGM Studios Theme Park** open at 8.30am. Closing hours vary widely from park to park, day to day and season to season. Check with Disney hotels or Disney information (407) 824-4321 for details.

In the parks, **breakfast and snack places** keep the same hours as the parks: **restaurants** open at 11.30am or 12 noon. Elsewhere, breakfast is served from 6 or 7am, lunch from 11am and dinner from as early as 5pm until 10 or11pm.

Business hours are from 8 or 8.30am to 5 or 5.30pm. **Shops** open from 9 or 10am. Closing hours vary from 5.30 to 9pm (and some supermarkets and convenience stores are open round the clock).

Typhoon Lagoon and **River Country**: usually open at 10am and close at 5pm (later in summer).

Discovery Island: open from 10am to 5pm.

Pleasure Island: clubs and entertainment open at 7pm and close at 2am (the shops are open from 10am).

Universal Studios: open at 9am: closing time varies.

134 **Sea World**: open from 9am to 8pm (8.30am to 9pm in summer).

PETS

Pets may *not* be taken into the theme parks, which operate kennels for pets near the entrance to each park. In many places, dogs are not allowed to run free, and they are usually barred from beaches, hotels, restaurants, food shops and public transport.

PHOTOGRAPHY and VIDEO

Camera shops sell film, but drugstores and supermarkets supply the same – at discount prices. A 2-hour printing service is available in major theme parks and elsewhere. If you are on a short visit, wait until you are home to develop slide film because it may take longer than you think. Don't store film anywhere in the car; it will get so hot in the sun that it may be damaged. Airport security X-ray machines are safe for normal film, whether exposed or unused. Super-fast film may be affected and you should ask for separate inspection.

You can rent cameras and video-cameras for use on Disney property at photographic shops in each park. Video-tape is available for all types of cameras. Note that pre-recorded tapes bought in the US will not function on European systems (and vice versa); nor will the tapes you make on rented equipment (and conversion is expensive).

POLICE (See also EMERGENCIES on p.126)

City police are concerned with local crime and traffic violations, while Highway Patrol officers (also called State Troopers) ensure highway safety, and are on the lookout for people speeding or driving under the influence of alcohol or drugs. Walt Disney World has its own security force and road patrol. You'll find American police officers friendly and tolerant of mild transgressions by foreigners.

For emergencies, dial **911** (fire, police, ambulance).

POST OFFICES

The US postal service deals only with mail. Telephone and telegraph services are operated by other companies. Post your letters in the blue kerbside boxes. The buff-coloured ones in Main Street, USA are cleared by Disney personnel and the letters taken to a post office. You can buy stamps from City Hall in the Magic Kingdom, and from machines in post office entrance halls after hours (there's also a post office at the Crossroads at Lake Buena Vista shopping centre).

Post office hours are from 8am to 5pm, Monday to Friday, from 8am to 12 noon on Saturday.

Poste restante (general delivery). You can have mail marked 'General Delivery' sent to you care of the main post office of any town. The letters will be held for one month. Take your passport or some other form of ID with you when you go to collect it.

PUBLIC HOLIDAYS

If a holiday, such as Christmas Day, falls on a Sunday, banks and most stores close on the following day.

New Year's Day	1 January
Martin Luther King Jr Day	Third Monday in January
Washington's Birthday *	Third Monday in February
President's Day	February (moveable)
Memorial Day	Last Monday in May
Independence Day	4 July
Labor Day	First Monday in September
Columbus Day *	Second Monday in October
All Saints's Day	1 November
Veterans' Day	11 November
Election Day	November (moveable)
Thanksgiving	Fourth Thursday in November
Christmas Day	25 December

RADIO and TV

Numerous AM and FM radio stations broadcast pop, rock and country-and-western music, but each city has at least one classical station.

Every hotel room has a television carrying many channels, some 24-hour. Florida news begins around 6pm, national and international news at 6.30 or 7pm, and is broadcast on several networks. Many hotels carry CNN Network, which broadcasts news around the clock.

Commercial American television aims to appeal to the largest possible number, and the amount of advertising tends to annoy those who are not familiar with it. The exceptions are PBS (Public Broadcasting Service) channels which screen music, drama and educational programmes including imports. Special-interest shows and films are aired on cable channels (some are piped free into hotel rooms; some you have to pay for).

RELIGION

There are Catholic services at Disney's Polynesian Resort (Sundays at 8am and 10.15am) and a Protestant service there at 9am. Elsewhere, Saturday newspapers often list the scheduled church services of the following day, with details of visiting preachers. Besides Catholic, Episcopalian, Presbyterian and Methodist churches, you'll see many branches of fundamentalist and southern Baptist denominations. Jewish services are held at the synagogues in Orlando.

SMOKING

Smoking is not permitted on any attraction, ride or waiting area in theme parks. Most restaurants have designated smoking and non-smoking areas – you will be asked which you prefer. Non-smoking rooms are available at many hotels – ask when you make your reservation or when you check in.

TELEPHONES

American telephone companies are efficient and reliable. Phones are found in the streets, at service stations, in shopping plazas, restaurants and most public buildings. Directions explaining how to use them are posted on the instrument. To make a local call, lift the receiver, put 25¢ in the slot, wait for the dialling tone, then dial the seven-digit number. The operator will automatically inform you of any additional charge, so have some change ready.

For local directory inquiries dial 411. For local operator assistance, and for help within the same area code, dial 0. For directory assistance in another area, dial 1, then the area code, then 555 1212.

Long-distance calls may be dialled direct from a pay phone if you follow the directions. The prefix 1- is usually needed. If you don't know the correct area code, dial 00 for assistance. Long-distance calls cost more from a pay-phone than from a private one. The international access code is 011, followed by the country code.

Charges are listed in the introduction to the white pages of the telephone directory, with information on person-to-person (personal), collect (reverse-charge) and credit card calls. Some companies no longer accept major credit cards. Numbers with an 800- prefix are toll-free, although hotels add a charge. They may also begin charging after a certain number of 'rings' even though there has been no answer, so don't hold on too long.

Fax. You can send faxes from larger hotels and from office service bureaux in some shopping malls.

Telegrams. American telegraph companies offer domestic and overseas services, as well as domestic telex facilities, and are listed in the YELLOW PAGES. You can telephone the telegraph office, dictate the message and have the charge added to your hotel bill, or dictate it from a coin-operated phone. A letter telegram (night letter) costs about half the rate of a normal telegram. Remember that the UK has only a telemessage service (copies are delivered with the mail).

TIME DIFFERENCES

The US has four time zones; Florida (like New York) is on Eastern Standard Time (EST). Between April and October Daylight Saving Time is adopted and clocks move ahead one hour. The following chart shows the time in other cities in *winter* at noon in Florida:

Los Angeles	**Orlando**	London	Sydney
9am	**noon**	5pm	4am
Sunday	**Sunday**	Sunday	Monday

Dates in the US are often written differently from the European day/month/year system; for example, 1/6/95 means 6 January 1995.

TIPPING

In many restaurants waiters and waitresses earn most of their salary from tips; often they are paid little else. Cinema or theatre ushers and filling-station attendants are not tipped. Some suggestions:

Tour guide	10-15%
Hairdresser/barber	15%
Hotel porter	50¢-$1, per bag (minimum $1)
Taxi driver	15%
Waiter	15–20%

TOILETS / RESTROOMS

Euphemisms are an American pastime; thus you can use a wide range of expressions to avoid, at all costs, calling a toilet a toilet: 'restroom', 'powder room', 'bathroom', 'comfort station' – the list is endless. Theme parks have many public toilets, marked 'restrooms'. Elsewhere you can find them in restaurants, railway stations and large stores. Most are free, but in some places you must deposit a dime or quarter. If there's an attendant, leave a tip.

TOURIST INFORMATION

For information prior to arrival, write to one of the following: United States Travel Service, 22 Sackville Street, London W1X 2EA; tel. (071) 439-7433; Florida Division of Tourism in Europe, 18-24 Westbourne Grove, London W2 5RH; tel. (071) 727-1661; The Walt Disney Company, 31-32 Soho Square, London W1V 6AP; tel. (071) 439-1962; Disney World, Box 10,000, Lake Buena Vista, FL 32830-1000, USA; tel. (407) 824-4321.

There can be few places in the world with so much printed tourist literature. Information is dispensed from welcome stations on the main entry routes to Florida, but the chief source of tourist information in any town or resort is the local chamber of commerce office.

In Disney hotels, TV channels 5, 7 and 10 give information, and you can telephone 824-4321 for yet more information.

TRANSPORT (See also Airports on p.117, Car Rental on p.118, Driving on p.123 and Getting to Orlando on p.126)
The Walt Disney World Resort transportation system is complex, as are the rules about who can use it. They include those staying in Disney accommodation, at the Plaza hotels, or those carrying Four or Five-Day passes. Additionally, those with Magic Kingdom tickets can use the monorail or ferry to get to its entrance.

Disney buses connect all areas within Walt Disney World. They carry colour codes and prominent signs.

The **Disney World Monorail** links Disney's Magic Kingdom resorts with the Magic Kingdom and the EPCOT Center.

Ferries operate between the TTC and the Magic Kingdom entrance; between the Contemporary Resort and Magic Kingdom, River Country and Discovery Island; and between the Swan, Dolphin and Yacht and Beach Club Resorts and Disney-MGM Studios.

Taxis always carry a roof sign. Most taxis have meters, and the rates are generally painted on the doors. A few taxis wait at theme parks and other attractions towards closing time. Otherwise, you will have **140** to telephone (consult the Yellow Pages under *Taxicabs*).

WEIGHTS and MEASURES

(For fluid and distance measures see DRIVING on p.123.)

The United States is one of the last countries in the world to change officially from the imperial to the metric system. However, Americans under 25 years have only been taught the metric system.

Temperature

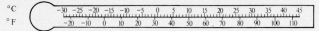

Length

Weight

grams	0	100	200	300	400	500	600	700	800	900	1 kg
ounces	0	4	8	12	1 lb	20	24	28	2 lb		

YOUTH HOSTELS

The US is not well endowed with youth hostels, although some budget hotels make rooms available to International YHA members at a large discount. There is no age limit. For further information, write to the American Youth Hostel Association, National Campus, Delaplane, VA 22025.

Index

Where more than one page reference is given, the one in **bold** is the main entry listed.